Fingerstyle
Guitar

LESSONS IN
TECHNIQUE
& CREATIVITY

by Brian Gore

Backbeat
Books
San Francisco

Published by Backbeat Books
600 Harrison Street, San Francisco, CA 94107
www.backbeatbooks.com
email: books@musicplayer.com

An imprint of the Music Player Network
Publishers of *Guitar Player*, *Bass Player*, *Keyboard*, *EQ*, and other magazines
United Entertainment Media. Inc.
A CMP Information company

CMP
United Business Media

Distributed to the book trade in the US and Canada by
Publishers Group West, 1700 Fourth Street, Berkeley, CA 94710

Distributed to the music trade in the US and Canada by
Hal Leonard Publishing, P.O. Box 13819, Milwaukee, WI 53213

Cover design by Tim Haselman
Composition by Michael Cutter

ISBN-13: 978-0-87930-812-4
ISBN-10: 0-87930-812-5

Printed in the United States of America

05 06 07 08 09   5 4 3 2 1

CONTENTS

INTRODUCTION

This book draws from a broad palette to teach fingerstyle guitar, and integrates techniques borrowed from folk, rock, classical, and jazz. Exercises are provided for fundamental and advanced techniques, which include left- and right-hand fret work, harmonics, slapping, and percussion produced on the guitar's strings and body. Mastering the exercises should help players develop valuable skills for composition and for interpreting the music of others. I have included some of my own music to contextualize the techniques.

Fingerstyle Guitar: Lessons in Technique & Creativity provides an overview of effective practice routines, covers compositional structure, and suggests strategies for tackling both alternate- and standard-tuned pieces. The presentation is "intuition based," requiring little harmonic knowledge or music education to assimilate. Wherever possible, I have also included perspectives from my compatriots in International Guitar Night. International Guitar Night is North America's premier forum for performing guitar composers. Many of the world's best players, from various walks of musical life, have performed in our productions. I'm proud that several IGN artists, including Pierre Bensusan, Peter Finger, Laurence Juber, and several other renowned fingerstylists have been interviewed for this book.

Slapping, tapping, two-handed fret work, and percussion add new dimensions to composition, but they are not as otherworldly as one may suspect. Once you get the hang of these unconventional techniques, they are easy to master. However, they are often overused or used out of context. Being able to articulate a melody—and being adept with basic hammer-ons, pull-offs, and accents—is the more essential skill. A great song needs a good melody, and everything else should support it.

One key to an effective performance is knowing a song inside and out, so we will explore visual memorization, kinetic memorization, song analysis, and practice with a metronome. Beyond formal preparation and study, knowing the true nature of the performance setting is also crucial. It's natural to be excited before a performance—and just as natural to confuse that excitement with nervousness. Both composition and performance are about transmitting thoughts and feelings through music to an audience. If you prepare right, and learn to cope with the potential for some imperfection, it will be easier for the music to flow. *Fingerstyle Guitar* can help you achieve this musical promise.

I'd like to thank my dear friends Peppino D'Agostino and Andrew York for the years of support and informal guidance they have provided in the development of my musical voice.

Without them and the scores of other players I have worked with in International Guitar Night, this book would not be possible. I'd also like to thank my booking agent, Herschel Freeman, and road manager Richard Rice for their support. Thanks as well to Backbeat Books Editor Richard Johnston, who has shown me much patience and kindness during the year it took to develop the text. Finally, a special word of thanks goes to Rich Maloof, the Development Editor on this project. Rich truly is one of a kind, and his experience as a music book author himself has proven indispensable.

— Brian Gore

For more information on the International Guitar Night, please visit www.theguitarnight.com.

A Note on Fingering

There are two basic strategies for managing the performance of a composition with the right hand: *(pp) p–i–m* (the thumb and first two fingers), and *(pp) i–m–a* (the thumb and first three fingers). It's possible to perform basic folk, rock, and country songs using *pim*. But most compositions utilize a combination of the two techniques. Most fingerstyle guitarists are self-taught and evolve into the use of the ring finger. This book provides the tools for you to manage the same transition, and discusses the relationship of hand position, attack, nail length, and nail shape. For those already comfortable with use of the ring finger, the book provides extensive tips and exercises you can use to develop flexibility in tone, accenting, and volume control.

CHAPTER 1

HOLDING THE GUITAR

SEATED POSITIONS

Cross-Legged Positions.

In Figure 1, Pierre Bensusan rests the guitar across the right side of his hip, folding his right leg over his left knee in a "half lotus" position. This is an alternate position for Pierre.

Figure 1

An alternative to the half-lotus position is the cross-legged position. In the cross-legged position, the upper part of the right leg is crossed over and rests on the left, with the guitar resting on top of the right hip.

Flat-Footed Positions.

Figure 2 shows Laurence Juber as he would sit in the flat-footed position, with the guitar resting on the top of his right leg. Note that the guitar is positioned so that the guitar neck is at a very slight angle to the legs rather than parallel to them. This position creates more space for left forearm movement.

Figure 2

An alternative to the flat-footed position involves using a foot riser to support either the left (classical position) or right leg. Pierre Bensusan, for example, plays with a foot riser supporting his right leg. Instead of using a riser, Laurence Juber will sometimes raise his right leg slightly by placing his right foot on the rung of a stool.

Seated, with Guitar Strap.

Figure 3 shows Martin Taylor playing in the seated position using a guitar strap. The guitar rests between his legs, with only a small portion of the guitar's back resting against his abdomen and chest. The strap assists him in propping the guitar up between his legs.

Figure 3

An alternative to this position is to use the guitar strap to help approximate the relationship of the neck and soundhole found in the classical position. When using a strap to accomplish this goal, nearly all the surface of the guitar back touches the abdomen and chest, and the hand can be placed so that fingers have a 45- to 60-degree angle of attack across the strings.

STANDING POSITIONS

Figures 4–6 illustrate two variations on standing positions. In Figure 4, Don Ross illustrates the typical position used in implementing his "heavy wood" style of

Figure 4

playing. Borrowing from electric guitar, the distance between Don's head and the lower half of the guitar body is a bit longer than it would be if he were seated. The same is true with Laurence Juber in Figure 5: the neck of the guitar in LJ's standing position is a bit higher than when seated. This approach is flashy looking, and is also more accommodating to playing with a flatpick.

Figure 6 illustrates Peppino D'Agostino's approach to playing while standing. In this case, the guitar strap is adjusted so that the distance between Peppino's head, the guitar neck, and the soundhole are relatively the same, regardless of whether he is seated or standing.

Figure 5

Figure 6

HOLDING THE GUITAR: THE MOST FUNDAMENTAL RELATIONSHIP

"I don't really think of it as holding the guitar. I aim for a more organic, synergistic relationship."
—Laurence Juber

Unlike classical guitar, many options for holding the guitar are open to the fingerstyle guitarist. What's right for one person may not be right for another. You have to adopt a way of holding the guitar that is the most comfortable for you. You can only find your own way by trying out various positions.

If you already have a preferred way (or ways) of holding the guitar, it may still pay to try something new. If you don't have a comfortable position yet, find one now! You may, in time, decide to vary how you hold the guitar. That's okay—and in fact, I recommend it. Pierre Bensusan alters his position periodically to offset the physical effects of playing in one position all the time, which is an excellent idea. Here are some insights provided by Pierre regarding his use of a foot riser, which is widely used by classical guitarists:

> I usually rest my right foot on a foot riser, on which I place a volume pedal. [I do] this in order to have my guitar at the right height for an accurate balancing movement between both arms and hands. I do sometimes cross legs for the same reasons. I like this less because it gives to my lower back a torso movement which, if repeated every day, will really damage my back and all the rest, ultimately.

Regardless of your position, give yourself some "wiggle room" to work with, as some range of movement is required by regular breath and hand work. Range of movement also helps reduce the risk of developing chronic physical conditions from remaining in fixed positions for countless hours of performance and practice. Most importantly, be comfortable. The more comfortable you are, the easier it will be for you to be expressive with the instrument.

Posture

One's posture can reveal a surprising amount about personality, habits, and even concerns. Take some time to look at yourself in a mirror as you hold your guitar. If you are intense or thoughtful, you may find you resemble Rodin's famous sculpture, *The Thinker*, when you hold the guitar. If you are introspective or shy, you may find that your head is bent when you play, such as to hide your face, or that your shoulders are hunched protectively over the top of the guitar.

The characteristics behind these physical expressions may have served you well in life, but they may present problems when it comes time to play guitar. They might create equal tendencies, such as lurching too far forward over the instrument or bending your upper back to the left or right, which could result in physical injury over the long run, or limit your flexibility and dexterity as a player. If you are comfortable with an "unbalanced" playing position, you still need to be aware of its long-term pitfalls. It may be worthwhile for you to rehabituate over time, through practice, to a position where the shoulders are even, and the back is more upright and straight.

This is what Pierre Bensusan has to say about the posture he's evolved when playing guitar:

> I am very aware of damages caused by wrong postures. I cannot really say that the position I use when performing would be a good exemple. In concert, I chronically sit in a sort of fetal position, with my mouth or right ear lined over the side of the instrument. I play like this in order to really hear the bass tones. This is not really good, though. When I play for myself and practice, I have a much more conventional position. Nowadays, live, I am alternating between this position and a more straight and "up" position where I look at people, especially when I sing.

Balance and Tension

Playing guitar is all about maintaining optimum balance and managing tension. An optimal performance condition is achieved when your physical balance is maximized and extra tension—both physical and emotional—is minimized. This requires finding the path of least resistance.

Our center of gravity affects how we manage tension, so it's helpful first to understand the body's relation to gravity, or balance, in your preferred playing position. For example, playing with the left shoulder lower than the right can lead to a shift in your center of gravity, with more of your body's weight being supported by the left hip and buttocks. Extra tension is required if you then hunch your right shoulder to bring the right hand to the soundhole. Lowering your head or bending forward with the chest likewise shifts weight towards your legs and feet, rather than centering it in the hips and buttocks.

Finding the position that's comfortable for you may involve establishing an initial center of gravity that does have you leaning toward one side. More than likely than not, you'll find yourself pivoting slightly between various positions rather than staying in one fixed place while you play. In the end, only you know what's right for you, so ask yourself: *Is the way I hold the instrument facilitating my ability to effectively express myself musically through the guitar? If not, what can I do to change that?* There is nothing good or bad or right or wrong about the way your posture relates to the instrument. But you put yourself at an advantage by locating your center of gravity and trying to maintain as much possible balance in your preferred positions during practice and performance.

You want to be able to apply exactly the amount of tension to the strings with your hands that is required to express the music; ideally, nothing more and nothing less. "Extra tension" includes thoughts that interrupt concentration when you play. When you practice, your attention should be fully present on the music, and you should be conscious of your goals. If your mind wanders, put down the guitar and take a few deep breaths, or work on something else until you are ready to focus. If you practice in front of a mirror, you'll note that posture often changes when the mind wanders or when you are frustrated or anxious. If you feel or observe that your center of gravity has shifted, take a break. Then, resume working on your music in a more balanced, centered physical position and mental state.

Most of us hold extra physical tension in our bodies; for example, in our neck, shoulders, or lower back. This extra tension is, in part, a physical reaction to stress, frustration, and anxiety. Playing guitar is incredibly challenging and can exacerbate physical tension. Learning to identify the places in the body where we hold this type of extra tension is a very important step in learning to manage it. Take note of where you hold extra tension when you play and what thoughts trigger the tension. You may discover that you clench your jaw when you are attempting a particular passage, for example, or that your neck becomes tense when you are frustrated. Stretching, breathing, and autosuggestion (affirmations and visualizations) can be used to mitigate this tension and improve your concentration. These techniques are discussed in greater detail in Chapter 11.

Optimizing Balance and Avoiding Injury
This cannot be stressed enough: Pain does not equal gain. If you are hurting *anywhere* when playing guitar, *stop playing until the pain goes away.*

Here are a few more words on the matter from Pierre Bensusan:

> The classical position would be the best but it's too late for my back to switch. When I do, it causes pains after 15 minutes. The ideal would be to find a position where both shoulders are on the same line, well balanced, both feet flat on the ground, the lower back all relieved, and the guitar carried by a system of belts so that we don't have to carry it but just manipulate it. The right arm not too high, so that the blood can circulate and feed the hand, and letting the

right hand free above the strings anywhere between the end of the neck and the saddle.

There is no ideal world, so we must make trade-offs. But, if you play in an unbalanced position, the best approach for physical health and musical synergy is to wean yourself of the habit. There is really no way around it: conventional approaches to holding the instrument for fingerstyle guitar are taxing on the body. They encourage players to twist their back and lean over the guitar. Guitarists can develop physical problems as a result, including sciatica, thoracic outlet syndrome, and carpal tunnel. You can mitigate these problems by optimizing a balanced posture as much as possible. Doing so also facilitates playing. The challenges to optimizing balance are as much mental as they are physical. Accordingly, here are ten suggestions for optimizing posture and addressing psychological and physical pitfalls.

- *Vary your seated position from time to time.*
  Alternating between the half-lotus, cross-legged and flat-footed position is healthy for the leg joints and can help diffuse lower back tension. Playing in either of the crossed-legged positions is taxing on the lower back and can irritate the sciatic nerves.

- *Distribute weight evenly between left and right sides while playing seated.*
  Bending forward shifts the weight of the upper body towards the legs and feet; bending backward shifts the weight towards the buttocks; and bending to one side or the other will shift the weight of the upper body more to the left or right. Keeping the weight of the upper body evenly distributed between both hips/buttocks encourages playing from a more centered, erect position, which maximizes balance.

- *Keep shoulders even. Don't hunch. Avoid playing with a bent upper back or twisted spine.*
  Playing with one shoulder lower than the other can produce chronic neck and shoulder tension. Hunching or collapsing shoulders creates chronic tension as well. Playing with one shoulder farther back than the other can result in a twist in the spine, encouraging chronic lower back pain. You should have a sense of the spine resting evenly between your two hips when seated.

- *Keep the head erect. Keep your neck straight and your head upright.*
  Craning the neck to look down while playing is stressful on both the neck and shoulders. Instead, try to direct your eyes down toward the guitar while moving your head as little as possible.

- *Use a guitar strap.*
  I recommend playing with a guitar strap, as illustrated in Figure 3. Place the pin for one end of the strap on the side of the upper bout, about two inches above the neck. (Note

that some guitars will already have a pin in this position or elsewhere.) Adjust the guitar strap so that the guitar rests lightly or just above both legs. I have found this way of playing the guitar to be easiest on my back and shoulders, with the most possible space for both arms and hands.

- *Stay centered, with your mind focused on the music.*
  Practice periodically in front of a full-length mirror, and "center yourself" physically using the first five suggestions above as a guide. Take a few deep breaths, and clear your mind. Look at yourself in the mirror, and notice your posture. Remind yourself briefly of your goal with the instrument before you begin to practice.

  If your mind wanders while you are playing, stop. Take a look at your posture. How has it changed? Take note of the intruding thoughts. Were you anxious? Frustrated? How might your posture be expressing these thoughts? Center yourself before returning to the task at hand, then begin again.

- *Take note of where you hold tension in your body. When you become tense or stressed, take a break, breathe, and stretch.*
  Chronic physical tension inhibits effective playing, and more often than not is exacerbated by playing in a position of imbalance. If physical tension is persistent, consider getting regular massage or visiting a chiropractor. Regular long baths or "spa days" are also highly recommended.

- *Use positive thinking, affirmation, and visualization to combat frustration, stress, and anxiety.*
  See Chapter 11 for more on psychological techniques for maximizing performance and practice.

- *Develop an effective warm-up routine and stretch regularly during practice.*
  Warm-up and stretching routines are provided in Chapter 11.

POSTURE: AN INTERVIEW WITH LAURENCE JUBER

It looks to me like your right shoulder is a bit further back than your left when you hold the guitar while seated, and that your left shoulder is lower than your right. Such a position would result in a slight twist to the right of the upper portion of the upper back, as well as a tilt to the left. Is this a correct assessment?

Don't base anything on album cover photos [*laughs*]. My shoulders are level. My upper body is turned slightly to the right. My back is generally straight. The points of contact are the inside of the upper right arm and the right thigh. The right forearm is free. Often the right leg ankle sits on the left knee to raise the guitar slightly, to expedite left-hand barre chords.

The guitar body is held vertically [i.e., not tilted back —Ed.] and sits at about a 30-degree angle away to the right of the body, with the headstock free to move forward in an arc of a further 15 degrees or so.

Has your body position in relation to the guitar ever caused you any physical problems, and if so, what did you do about them?

I occasionally see an Alexander practitioner (www.alexandertechnique.com) for a posture "tune-up," and will go to the chiropractor at the first sign of a misalignment. Often the chair or stool at a concert will require some slight modification of my posture. For example, with my right heel on the rung of a stool, I can raise my right leg slightly.

Have you ever found yourself having to renegotiate the way you hold the instrument in order to facilitate technical alacrity or to mitigate physical problems?

I really don't think of it as "holding" the instrument—I aim for a more organic, synergistic relationship. I do allow for a wide variation in posture. For example, to accommodate long stretches I will drop my left elbow, in order to arch my wrist, and I'll lean forward so that the lower waist of the guitar pivots on my right thigh, and the upper body follows. I try to avoid rounding my back, as that can cause discomfort. Avoiding sugar and yeast in my diet seems to help avoid muscle problems, plus I take the occasional yoga class and do some light stretching to stay relatively limber.

When you stand with the guitar, I notice that the bottom half of the guitar is much lower than it would be if you were in the seated pose with the instrument. This looks very cool, and reminds me of how an electric guitarist would hold his/her instrument. Does that position also facilitate soloing with a flat pick or some other aspect of performance?

Dropping the lower bout allows me to maintain the same right-hand position as when I sit. However, if I play standing and sul ponticello [on the bridge], I'll tend to drop my right wrist—otherwise, it's hard to maintain control. Also, for flatpicking I like where it puts the sweet spot: if the guitar is more even, I end up picking too close to the bridge. That can change depending on the guitar, though. Rosewood has a bigger bottom end and will stay sweet closer to the bridge, so there is some flexibility.

CHAPTER 2

HAND PLACEMENT

FINDING YOUR OWN WAY

In fingerstyle guitar, appropriate hand placement is just as much of a journey of discovery as holding the instrument. However, many self-taught players develop forms of hand placement that don't honor the delicate anatomy of the hand, wrist, and arm. As Figures 2-1 and 2-2 illustrate, the tendons that move the fingers pass through a tight inlet called the carpal tunnel, and are attached to very fine musculature. It's easy for these muscles and tendons to be overexerted, resulting in inflammation and nerve damage.

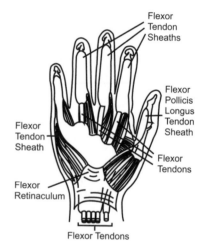

Figure 2-1

It pays to honor anatomy! Finding your own way requires the development of guidelines for yourself that help minimize muscular resistance and maximize dexterity. It's really very simple: avoid turning the joints in any direction that might cause excess torque or impede the free flow of movement. For example, it's very common for folk players to plant their right hand behind the bridge of the guitar, resulting in an upward turning of the wrist. Another common technique involves planting the pinky on the guitar top. These techniques (habits, really) not only impede your ability to make use of dynamic qualities in the guitar, but limit finger mobility, minimizing the effectiveness of the attack. Bending the wrist downward or upward creates undue strain on the tendons in the carpal tunnel, decreasing mobility and also creating the risk of injury.

Ignoring these considerations will inhibit finger mobility; even worse, it can lead to irritation of

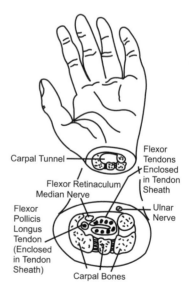

Figure 2-2

the nerves and pain in the joints. Try to keep the wrist even, not rotating it too much in one direction or the other. This idea applies to both the right and left hands alike. Keeping the idea of minimizing resistance and maximizing dexterity in mind will preserve your physical well-being and also help you play more fluidly—a win-win, to be sure.

If you are a beginner, follow the recommendations provided in this chapter. Even if you are a more seasoned player, try to rehabitate your approach for the sake of your hands and joints. You'll play better, and in a way that's healthy for you.

THE FRETBOARD HAND: ASSUMING THE POSITION

Use the following three-step approach to "assume the position" for the left hand:

1. Drop the fretboard hand to your side. While it's resting there, feel the weight of gravity and release all the energy and tension from your hand. Take a look at your hand and wrist. Note the slight natural arch in the lower wrist, due to the extension of the thumb.

2. Bring the hand up just under the neck at the first position on the guitar (the first four frets) without altering the hand-to-wrist relation when your arm was at your side.

3. Place the thumb so that it rests on the neck directly behind the second finger. Again, the wrist position should vary as little as possible from when your arm was at your side. See Figures 2-3, 2-4, and 2-5.

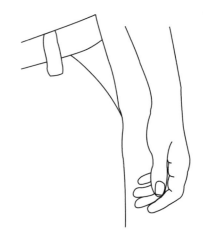

Figure 2-3

The Thumb of the Fretting Hand
If you follow the guidelines for dexterity and resistance, and use the above suggestions as a stepping stone for developing an optimal fretboard-hand position, the front thumb pad and middle thumb joint should receive the bulk of the application pressure required to fret notes. You will not use the *side* of the thumb or the *tip* of the thumb as a basic position, since either will result in unnecessary torque to the thumb joints. You can see, as well, that it's wise to avoid cradling the neck of the guitar in the palm, as this would create unnecessary bending

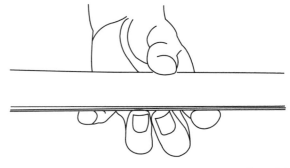

Figure 2-4

of the wrist which would impede the movement of
tendons through the carpal tunnel.

As with any positioning, there will be wiggle
room and some variation before you find your own
optimal position. For instance, folk musicians often
use the thumb for fretting the lowest string in standard tuning and the lowest two strings in *DADGAD*.
Employing this technique requires turning the wrist
away from the feet and cradling the neck in the palm.
It's helpful sometimes to move the arm forward and
bend the wrist a bit when attempting fingerings that
involve distances of more than four frets.

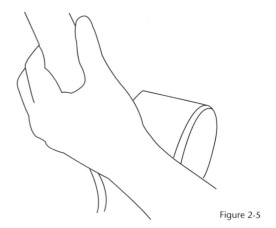

Figure 2-5

TWANG: RIGHT HAND, FOLK STYLE

Many different conventions exist in fingerstyle guitar for the positioning and placement of the
hand plucking the strings (or "soundhole hand"). They include:

- Resting the lower wrist on the bridge

- Planting the pinky just below the soundhole

- Planting the ring finger on the highest string

- Placing the hand over the strings in a "claw" formation

These conventions are often adopted because they seem easier than the alternative: the
classical guitar–influenced approach described below. Use of the above hand positions is
widespread, and has acculturated our ears to a certain "twangy" tone associated with folk,
blues, and country music. As such, these right-hand habits have played an important role in
the evolution of folk-based fingerstyle guitar technique.

If you feel comfortable, and you like the results, you may decide you want to adopt these
conventions as part of your style. It's perfectly legitimate to do so, and probably not impossible to produce a tone familiar and pleasing to your ear. That said, planting the wrist or finger
is an unnecessary and sometimes problematic crutch for many players. Such positions often
create more resistance and tension, as they often involve twisting the wrist. Thus, they require
more effort, not less, than the classically oriented approach.

CLANG: RIGHT HAND, CLASSICAL STYLE

I recommend positioning the hand in a way that approximates the classical convention: without
planting a finger below the soundhole or on a string, and keeping your wrist naturally straight.

1. Drop the soundhole hand to your side. While it's resting there, feel the weight of gravity and release all the energy and tension from your hand. Take a look at your hand and wrist. Note the slight natural arch in the lower wrist, due to the extension of the thumb.

2. Plant your fingers on the top three strings and your thumb on the lowest string without altering the hand-to-wrist relation when your arm was to your side. See Figures 2-6 and 2-7.

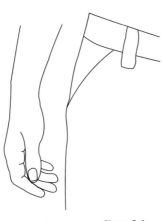

Figure 2-6

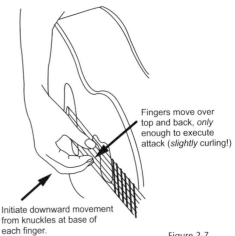

Fingers move over top and back, *only* enough to execute attack (*slightly* curling!)

Initiate downward movement from knuckles at base of each finger.

Figure 2-7

Using this classically oriented position is the first step in producing a round, "clangy" tone. The next section will explain how hand position and finger use account, in part, for tonal differences.

THE ANATOMY OF TWANG AND CLANG

Two factors account for the "twangy" tone often associated with folk traditions in fingerstyle guitar:

- The conventional folk hand positions encourage articulation of motion from the first two joints in the fingers (phalanges).
- Strings are plucked by getting the tips of right-hand fingers under the string and then pulling outward and upward.

The habit of bending the wrist upward and/or placing the wrist very close to the soundhole

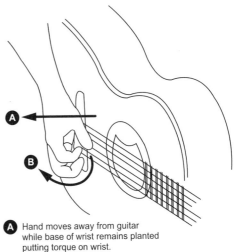

A Hand moves away from guitar while base of wrist remains planted putting torque on wrist.

B Fingers reach under the strings and pull up and back, as fingers curl.

Figure 2-8

contributes significantly to the approach. The fingers and the entire wrist must move in order to pluck the strings when the wrist has an upward bend (as is the case, for example, when the wrist is planted on the bridge). Placing the wrist very close to the soundhole results in a "claw" formation, limiting the motion of the fingers to only the first two joints when plucking the strings.

The classical style of hand placement lends itself to fuller tone when the strings are plucked using the following means of attack:

- Initiate the motion from the joints *at the base of each finger* (the knuckle).

- Pluck by moving the fingers over the top of the string and back.

Please note that this section is entitled "The Anatomy of Twang *and* Clang"—not "Twang *versus* Clang." There is nothing more refined, or better, about either method. Still, my recommendation is to adopt the classically oriented approach to the right hand, because it increases your options. In order to use it, the wrist has to be far enough above the soundhole to move from the knuckles. Even with your wrist floating above the strings at an ample distance, you can easily adjust your attack if you want to switch quickly to a folk-style attack for a twang tone.

HAND POSITIONS: AN INTERVIEW WITH DALE MILLER

Have you noticed that your positioning and use of the left hand has evolved over the years? If so, how?

Very early on, I realized the importance of a nice arch on my left-hand fingers to sound out the notes cleanly and to avoid touching adjacent strings. My left-hand positioning evolved to support this goal. After playing for a year or so I discovered alternating-bass fingerpicking. Songs like "Freight Train" taught me the importance of a strong left-hand pinky finger, and I spent a few months working on exercises to strengthen it. As the years passed I worked to control the strings by varying pressure for different tones. I developed a pretty good tremolo and string-bending technique.

I learned to play bottleneck slide about 20 years after first picking up the guitar. With a tube on my left-hand pinky I lost a flexible finger and gained a "bionic" digit. My pinky muscles, tendons, and ligaments were rendered immobile. This affected the adjacent fingers. I had to take it slow and easy for a while to avoid straining anything when chording with a slide on. When playing notes with the slide, I learned to keep a very loose wrist for tremolo effects.

Have you encountered any injuries that affected the agility of your left hand?

I've been lucky in the injury department. I've sprained a finger from time to time; once, interestingly enough, when I was guarding [fingerstylist] Duck Baker in a pickup half-court basketball game. I've also played to the point of developing tendon, muscle, and ligament soreness, but I've always been able to listen to my body's signals and recover by taking a couple of days off from playing. I think once or twice I actually had to stop playing for a week, but I was able to recover fully.

Learning slide was helpful for this. If I overplay nowadays, I go to playing slide, where almost all the movement is in the wrist and arm.

I've learned over the years to start slowly when practicing and not make difficult stretches until I'm well warmed up.

Is your left wrist generally straight, or are there times when you arch your wrist forward—or even backward—when you play?

One of my overriding rules in guitar playing is to minimize movement. The only time I can remember consciously thinking about my wrist position was after developing the bad habit of moving around my left elbow too much. I found I could put my fingers in the same place by moving my wrist instead of my elbow. I spent a few weeks relearning. These movements were more left and right than forward and back. Otherwise, I've always let my wrist go where it wants to in order to get a nice arch to my left-hand fingers, as I mentioned before. My wrist doesn't move that much, but I will arch it forward or backward or left or right. For slide playing, I keep an extremely loose wrist.

Regarding the position of your thumb on the back of the neck: Is it between the first two fingers, or closer to the nut? And, do you keep your thumb roughly parallel to the frets, or at a 90-degree angle to the neck? Or is it angled more to the left? At what angle do you keep your thumb in relationship to the neck?

I move from 45 to 75 degrees. In general, the farther up the neck I go, the lower the angle. As I mentioned, I've always let the thumb fall where it wants as I go for a nice arch with the fingers.

When playing notes with the slide, my thumb varies from making no contact with the neck to barely touching, and it's close to 90 degrees.

Do you ever use your thumb to fret the lowest strings on the guitar? Just the low E *string, or also the* A?

I love to use the thumb for a low G note on the 6th string in standard tuning. This can put some strain on the left hand, but it allows for some extremely cool techniques, like moving double-stops on the 2nd and 3rd strings. I'll even go up to the 7th fret with two fingers from this position. I also really like the *D/F♯* chord using the thumb for the 6th string. Higher up the neck, I'll keep my thumb down where it "belongs," with a few exceptions. I don't use my left-hand thumb on the 5th string, though I briefly experimented with the Reverend Gary Davis–style *C7* chord, where he plays low G and C notes on the 6th and 5th strings, freeing a finger to play a high G on the 1st string. [*Davis had evidently broken his thumb once, which made it easy for him to finger this chord. —DM*]

HAND POSITIONS: AN INTERVIEW WITH JIM NICHOLS

How has your positioning and use of the left hand evolved over the years?

I haven't noticed any change in left-hand position, but I have tried to strengthen my left ring finger—it is lazy and weak, and I tend to play single lines using only the other three fingers. Being self-taught, I didn't notice this technical flaw for many years. I sometimes play a few chromatic scales and also try to use that finger more when playing lines. The result of using only three fingers is you tend to play a bit sloppy and do a lot of sliding and slurring. If I am struggling to play a lick, I analyze my fingering to see if I can do it better or more efficiently.

Over the years I have had various bouts of tendinitis, carpal tunnel, arthritis, and aches and pains. I have managed to get through all of those problems with heat, cold, stretching, not practicing much (my general approach always), and avoiding the activities that caused the pain if possible (lots of hammering nails, running a chainsaw, too much wrist bending from reaching for low *F*'s on electric bass). A hand surgeon showed me some stretches, and said drink lots of water to lubricate the tendons.

Is your left wrist generally straight, or are there times when you would arch your wrist forward or even backward when you play?

Left wrist is usually straight but bends a little either way—not too much because it hurts eventually. I try to stay comfortable when playing.

Is the location of your thumb on the back of the neck behind or in between the first two fingers, at roughly a 90-degree angle with the neck? Or is the thumb angled more to the left? When, if ever, does this position of the thumb, relative to the fingers, change for you?

I do use my thumb to grab the first two low bass strings—it is an old Atkins and Travis trick, and it is also good for jazz chords when you need to sound big. However, it is hard on the hand to do it a lot—too much stretching, and it locks your hand around the neck and kind of restricts your movement, so I do it sparingly. My left thumb mostly slides along the edge of the neck, a little bit down from the edge of the fingerboard, in basically the same natural position your hand is in when it isn't doing anything. In this position, the thumb is a little behind the other fingers and angled up towards the headstock a little bit. It only acts as a guide along the neck and only changes for the bass note thing.

CHAPTER 3

THE HOLY GRAIL: TONE PRODUCTION

THE EVOLUTION OF TONE

Fingerstyle guitar tone has evolved primarily from players of bluegrass, folk, jazz, and impressionist (or "new acoustic") styles. Impressionist artists in particular have played an important role in integrating technique from classical and Latin American music, while also tapping into bluegrass, folk, and jazz.

The trend towards technical diversity in fingerstyle guitar began in the 1960s, with the work of John Fahey in the United States and John Renbourn in Europe. Their groundbreaking efforts to integrate classical, jazz, and non-Western influences into an essentially folk-based style gave birth to a new generation of performing steel-string composers including Alex de Grassi, Pierre Bensusan, Michael Hedges, Peter Finger, and Peppino D'Agostino (to name a few). Each of these poets of the guitar has, in his own way, helped expand fingerstyle guitar technique into its current inclusive, highly eclectic state.

The "technical palette" presented in upcoming chapters is designed to help you develop a similarly inclusive and eclectic approach to performing and composing—especially pertaining to tone.

INFLUENCES ON TONE PRODUCTION

Tone production in fingerstyle guitar is more variant and complex than in classical guitar, because the range of influence and usable sounds is much more broad. For example, the sound of the plectrum (including thumb picks, finger picks, and flat picks) is a major influence on fingerstyle guitar sound. Equally important is the organic sound of fingernail on string—and the sound of playing with no nails. Dynamic range, the shifting of accents, and finger independence (all borrowed from classical technique) are just as important as blazing lead lines and loud presence (borrowed from pop and jazz) when it comes to fingerstyle.

So, there are many factors influencing tone production. A review of some particularly important influences, and recommendations for incorporating them, is provided here.

Hand Position and Angle of Attack

As discussed in Chapter 2, hand placement plays a crucial role in defining "twang" and "clang," since it impacts finger articulation. The position of the hand and the wrist also affects the angle of attack for the fingers, and influences how much nail or flesh is involved in the attack. However, it's difficult to isolate the exact role of hand placement, since nail length, nail shape, and use of plectrum or picks might also be at play.

Hand location also has influence on dynamics. For instance, placing the hand toward the front (neck side) of the soundhole produces a warm and soft sound, while placing it towards the back of the soundhole produces a bright and crisp sound.

I recommend that you place your hand over the soundhole so that there is enough room for the fingers to initiate a plucking motion from the knuckles. Don't twist the wrist in any direction. Keep the bottom part of the wrist parallel with the guitar top.

FINGER MOVEMENT AND ATTACK

Again, tone is influenced by the specific movement of the fingers. The sound is twangy when the strings are plucked with the first two joints in the fingers, and more clangy when the attack is initiated from the knuckles. Also, the tone is different if the strings are plucked upwards versus stroked from the top down; likewise, the tone differs if the finger moves out rather than back.

Note that the recommended method for attack described here is the same regardless of whether you play with nails or without. Most of the force for the motion of attack in the thumb and fingers should come from the knuckles. I recommend that you position the fingers so that they are at a 45- to 50-degree angle with the strings. This will help ensure an attack that involves a mix of skin and nail, assuming the fingernails aren't too long. Execute the attack so the fingers go over the top of the strings and back, not under and out.

Nails: Shape and Quality

The shape and the length of nails are major influences on tone. The sound of the finger on the strings will be different depending on whether the nail is shaped to the contour of the finger or is more pointed or angled. Nails of uneven length, with jagged edges or curves, also affect the overall quality of tone. Perfecting the quality of nails through effective use of emery boards, buffing boards, and fine-quality sandpaper also will influence tone.

Fingerstyle guitarists often worry too much about the length of their nails. The problem with nails usually isn't that they are too short—it's that they are unshaped or poorly maintained. I recommend you shape your nails with emery boards or fine sandpaper (600–800 grain) so that they follow the contour of your fingers. Aim for achieving a mix of nail and skin in your sound (see *Nail-to-Skin Ratio* below).

Nail-care products such as acrylic pastes, press-on nails, and nail strengtheners bring more of the "plectrum" sound into the fingers by hardening the nails and increasing their density and length. Use of such nail products also influences volume.

Nail-to-Skin Ratio

The ratio of nail to skin involved in the attack is a major influence on tone. Playing with longer nails will prevent skin from reaching the string, while shorter nails allow more flesh in the attack.

Classical players opt for nail length between one and two millimeters. Fingerstyle guitarists who play with nails typically play with longer nails. Long nails may get in the way when stopping a string or attacking an already ringing string, resulting in a buzz effect (since the string is vibrating on the nail rather than being muted by skin). For a sound that is more natural, try for a nail length that allows for a balance between nail and skin on the string.

Finger Independence

Finger independence extends beyond the free stroke and the rest stroke (introduced in an exercise at the end of this chapter). The accenting of notes through slight increases in volume is another very important feature of finger independence. Equally important is dynamic range and a balance in volume across the strings. Techniques for developing finger independence are provided throughout this book.

Plectrums

Tone (as well as technique) is greatly affected by the use of finger picks, thumb picks, and flat picks. Notes attacked with a pick will typically be bright and have a crisp attack that's difficult to emulate with bare fingers.

Many players use a thumb pick in place of the thumbnail but otherwise use fingernails. Some players will use a thumb pick only for certain songs, such as those requiring strumming or lead lines. Some fingerstyle jazz guitarists play lead lines and strumming patterns with a plectrum, but then store it between their fingers when plucking arpeggios.

PRESENCE

Presence is achieved when all the above influences on tone are brought to bear in a consistent manner. Ultimately, the strategic goal is to deliver the sound that is perfectly suited to your music.

For example, you have to decide whether to play with nails or not, or what mix of nails and flesh works best for you. If you decide to use acrylics or nail products, use them on all of your nails, not just some. The same is true for the use of finger picks and thumb picks: decide if, when, and how you are going to use them.

Likewise, you must be conscious of the method you choose for the attack. Reaching over and back produces a different kind of sound than reaching up and out when executing the attack. Being aware of these small differences, and deciding what your music requires, goes a long way towards defining your tone.

The locus of finger movement is very important. When you initiate the motion from the knuckle joints, you have more volume and control. You also maximize the economy of motion in a way that gives you the "biggest bang for your buck"; that is, you'll find that you are getting a richer, fuller sound. No matter how you decide to initiate the attack, a clean connection with buffed, well-shaped nails and consistent follow-through are major influences on presence in sound.

Volume is important to a lot of players. Many fingerstyle guitarists want a big sound, or want to really "push the instrument." Players who want more volume often make the false assumption that you have to play harder or more aggressively in order to get it. The result is often just a lot of extra string vibration and rattling that can be hard to control. When you play from the knuckle joints, you automatically get more power and control, which can translate into more volume. Other factors that influence volume include nail length, use of nail products, use of picks, and string gauge.

More important than volume is definition. Definition is achieved by playing articulately, that is, having enough finger independence to control variations in attack, timbre, volume, and accentuation.

THE INCEPTION OF SOUND: REST STROKE AND FREE STROKE

In fingerstyle guitar playing, three key elements inform the inception of sound:

- Planting the finger on the string

- Plucking the string

- Follow-through

There are two fundamental string strokes—the rest stroke and free stroke—that are at the core of creating a sound, and both employ planting, plucking, and follow-through.

In the rest stroke, the finger plucks a string and then rests on the adjacent lower string. Pluck by moving over and back (*not* up), and then follow through to rest just behind the point of attack on the adjacent lower string. Plucking and resting in this way helps make for rich, deep tone and sound duration.

Because you are not pulling up from under the string, the finger naturally pivots on the knuckle. Practicing the rest stroke can do wonders for the effort of rehabituating the fingers towards an approach that minimizes resistance and maximizes dexterity.

In the free stroke, the finger reaches over and back to pluck the string. Again, the pressure applied to the pluck comes primarily from the knuckle joints. However, in following through, the finger does not come to rest on the adjacent string; rather, the finger moves slightly in towards the palm. This requires a little motion in the first two joints of the finger in follow-through only.

When practicing, try alternating the rest stroke with the free stroke. Compare the differences in joint motion. Try to get the motion in the free stroke to approximate the naturally effective motion in the rest stroke as much as possible.

EXPERIMENTS IN TONE

String Stopping

For the first of our experiments, pluck a string with any finger. Once the string is vibrating, stop it with the nail of the same finger. Check it out: if you touch the string with your nail lightly, you will get a buzzing sound; stop it with your nail firmly and the result is a clicking sound.

Now pluck the string again. This time, stop it using the fleshy tip of your finger rather than the nail. Notice the difference? Sure, it's still possible to get a little buzz from a ringing string if touching too lightly with the fingertip. However, it's much easier to stop the sound of the ringing string without the buzz when using flesh instead of nail.

The point here is that strings are often still vibrating with the resonance of a previous note before they are plucked again. When you pluck an already vibrating string, you are actually stopping the ringing of the previous note, however briefly, before plucking the string again. If the nail is the first part of the finger involved in that stop, you will hear a click or a buzz.

Considering how often one is plucking the same string in succession, it's plain to see that nail noise can add up. The challenge is to figure out how to involve the fingertips rather than the nails in the inception of each new sound.

You can see how the length or shape of the nail can contribute to the click-and-buzz effect. Keeping the nails shorter reduces the likelihood that they'll get in the way when plucking an already vibrating string. However, if the nail is not shaped to the contour of the fingertips, the edges of the nail can catch on the string when planting. Many fingerstyle guitarists opt for longer nails because they feel it helps them get more volume, and when more nail is involved, the quality of the sound is more like a plectrum. Players like Don Ross and Peppino D'Agostino, who both opt for long nails, keep them angled or pointed so a significant amount of the front right portion of the fingertip can be involved in planting.

Angle of Attack

Now let's try a little experiment with the angle of attack as determined by the forearm and wrist. Plant the fingers on the highest three strings and the thumb on the 5th string. Each string should be touching the skin of each fingertip as close to the nail as possible. Pluck with each consecutive finger slowly—first with a rest stroke, then with a free stroke. Observe how the angle of the attack, and in turn the nature of the tone, is affected based on the forearm's position:

a) If the forearm is angled so that the wrist is closer to the top right-hand side of the soundhole, the fingers can have a 60- to 90-degree angle of attack to the strings. When plucking the strings from this angle, the sound should be sharp, like a plectrum, since more of the surface of the nail is traveling directly over the string when executing the attack.

b) If the forearm is angled so that the wrist is closer to the bridge, the fingers can have a 40- to 60-degree angle of attack to the strings. When plucking the strings from this angle, skin from the fingertip maintains contact and the nail slides over the top of the strings. The result is a rounder sound, since a more even percentage of skin and nail are involved in the attack.

Regardless of the forearm angle, the wrist should not be bent forward or back; the palm of the hand and the top of the guitar should be parallel planes.

Changing the angle of the wrist slightly by pointing it upwards brings more of the back of the nail into the attack, and sometimes the string will sit more deeply in the place between the nail and the fingertip. I call this "digging in."

Digging in and then plucking can be used to achieve a dramatic increase in volume and presence.

WHAT'S IT ALL MEAN, AND WHERE DO I GO FROM HERE?

We've just covered the elements involved in tone production. Very slight differences, such as nail length or the position of the forearm and wrist, can make a big difference in your sound. Again, what is most important is coming up with an angle of attack you are comfortable with and a basic tone you enjoy. It's likely this will involve experimentation until you develop an approach that works for you. It's all about presence. The more familiar you become with these influences, the sooner you're likely to achieve a sound that's all your own.

NAILING YOUR TONE: AN INTERVIEW WITH DON ROSS

When I last checked, you had pretty long nails, thickly coated with acrylic paste. Can you explain how this helps you do what you do with the guitar?

I've always had a very aggressive style, and my style is very funky and groove-based. For years I used a thumb pick and steel picks, but most of us know what the inherent shortfalls of metal picks are. About 15 years ago I started using artificial nails instead of picks, and it was nice to be able to pick upwards *and* downwards on the strings, as well as reach over and do percussive things with the right hand. I keep the nails relatively long because they make the aggressiveness a lot easier, but I still use a lot of flesh of the finger in combination with the nail to achieve my tone.

Did you ever maintain your nails in a different way? If so, how did you evolve this approach to your nails? How do you maintain them (filing, sanding, hacksawing, etc)?

The only solution that I have ever relied on is either professionally done salon nails (from the beauty parlor) or a nail kit that I buy at the pharmacy. Either way, I use a lot of filing to keep them the right length and shape.

When a string is still vibrating with the resonance of a previous note, we often get a "buzz" or "click" if the nail is used to pick the next note on that same string, instead of skin from the tip of the finger and then nail. Is this a problem for you? If so, how do you avoid it?

I do use a lot of rest-stroke technique that uses the flesh of the finger to stop the string before plucking again.

I recall that your right hand and wrist are placed so they are at about a 50° angle with the strings. Is this the case?

I think that I actually rest my forearm and wrist on top of the guitar, which provides stability—but which I know is not really a good habit—I get a lot of grief from classical players!—and then I'm able to keep my fingers and thumb "free floating" in front of the strings, without using any other stabilizing technique.

How does your hand/wrist placement affect the angle of attack for your fingers against the strings? Is most of the surface of your nail involved in the execution of the attack, or only the front portion?

Looking at the way my nails tend to wear from playing, it would seem that it's mostly the outside, or right side, of the nails that do the bulk of the work.

What finger joints are primarily/secondarily involved in your attack—the first two or the joints closest to the wrist?

I think I use a movement that employs a pretty free movement by the whole finger, as well as wrist movement for strumming attack.

How did you arrive at your particular approach toward executing the attack with your fingers?

No guru, no method, no teacher!

Are you reaching under the strings with the nails, then moving up when plucking the strings? Or are you reaching over the top and back?

I think it's the latter.

What gauge of strings do you use, and how important is the gauge of the strings to your tone?

I use medium gauge (.056 to .013) on my regular guitar, and a very heavy set on the baritone (.066 to .017), which consists of a custom-made sixth string and then the bottom five strings from a regular medium set for the top five positions [string 6, .066; string 5, .056; string 4, .045; string 3, .035; string 2, .026, string 1, .017]. In general, I feel my style is rendered pretty much impossible on lighter strings. I also really feel that the lighter the string, the less overall tone is possible. I like the richness of medium-gauge strings.

What role does amplification play in the production of your tone?

The pickups and internal mics I'm using these days lend less artificiality to the tone, but I still go for a "larger than life" kind of sound. So I still rely on that fat tone that is possible when I structure the tone onstage through pre-amplification and equalization.

You have a very big, "take no prisoners" kind of presence in your sound. What practical suggestions could you give to help initiates develop a presence similar to yours?

Well, I'm a large man, which lends a certain "muscularity" of tone to my playing in the first place. That, in combination with large guitars played with heavier strings, give that huge sound. It's hard to achieve similar results on a small guitar or with light strings. I also feel that my guitar setup allows me to "dig in" a bit more, which makes for a big, aggressive tone.

CHAPTER 4:

TONE COLOR AND DYNAMICS

TONE COLOR

One factor greatly affecting tone color is the position of the right hand over the soundhole. When music is played towards the front of the soundhole—closer to the neck—it is said to have a dark, warm, or soft sound. When it is played towards the back of the soundhole—closer to the bridge—it is said to have a bright, cool, or crisp sound.

Example 4-1, Tone Color, is comprised of variations on arpeggiated chords. Start with your right hand at the front of the soundhole and move slowly back; then move from the back toward the front again, and take note of the different shades of color. Maintain an equal balance of sound and volume in all four right-hand fingers used.

Ex. 4-1   Tone Color

example continues...

Ex. 4-1 continued

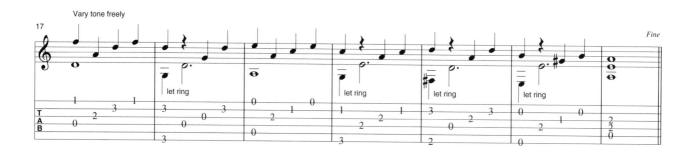

Effective usage of tone color requires the ability to keep the soundhole position mobile rather than fixed or rigid. Observe the position at the soundhole you've become habituated to. Avoid playing so close to the front of the soundhole that the fingers could touch the fretboard. Likewise, you may discover you're in the habit of playing more towards the back of the soundhole, especially if you plant your wrist on the bridge or your pinky on the guitar top. Wean yourself from these habits by finding the "sweet spot" on your guitar, where you get a great balance between dark and bright and warm and crisp. The exact position differs on every guitar, and sometimes with every player. It should be at a point not too close to the front of the soundhole, but not too far back either. Move forward from the "sweet spot" to get more dark warmth, and back to get more bright crispness.

DYNAMICS

In a general sense, "dynamics" is used to refer to the power (typically represented as volume) in your tone. It's a catchall term for many of the techniques discussed in the book. In Example 4-2, Dynamics, the term refers specifically to volume. Repeat each phrase twice, progressing from quiet to loud. Return to the beginning and repeat each phrase again, shifting this time from loud to quiet. Let each note ring as long as possible.

Ex. 4-2   Dynamics

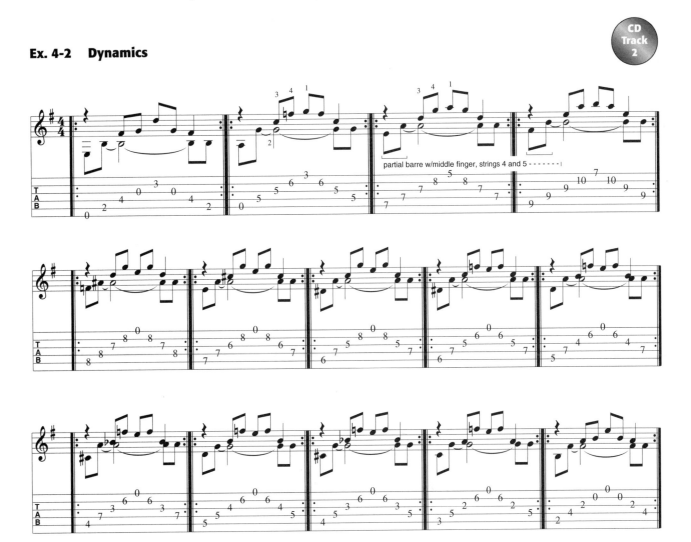

VARIATIONS

Tone color can be emphasized differently depending on volume. Try the dynamics exercise at various fixed positions above the soundhole, and take note of the differences. Try to vary the tone color by moving the right hand along the soundhole while increasing and decreasing the volume.

CHAPTER 5

STRING STOPPING AND SHIFTING ACCENTS

STRING STOPPING

There are three ways to stop a string from ringing:

    1) Lift the finger off the fretted note

    2) Press lightly on the plucked string with a left-hand finger

    3) Plant a right-hand finger on the plucked string

Left-Hand String Stop #1 (Example 5-1) utilizes left-hand fingers to stop the notes. In this exercise, the left-hand fingers remain in the *Em9* chord shape *until a finger is required to stop a string*. Each note is left ringing for its value and then stopped with the finger indicated at the rest sign. After the appropriate left-hand finger is used to stop a note, it is brought back to its root position in the *Em9* chord shape notated in measure 21.

Ex. 5-1   Left-Hand String Stop #1

Left-Hand String Stop #2 (Example 5-2) is trickier, but simpler to explain. In this exercise, the left-hand fingers fretting the notes are used to stop the ringing. Leave each note ringing for its value, and then stop each note by lifting up off the fretboard.

Ex. 5-2   Left-Hand String Stop #2

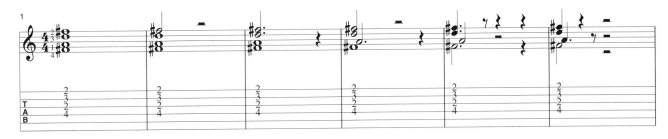

In the final exercise, Stop Ring (Example 5-3), each note is stopped completely *before* the next note is played. For this example we've used a staccato symbol on each notehead, though the note is not necessarily short. Rather, it sustains for its entire value but is stopped before the note that follows. There are three ways to approach the Stop Ring exercise:

1) Stop the string with the right-hand finger you used to initiate the sound (by planting)
2) Reach up or down with the 1st or 4th finger of the left hand to stop the note (this can apply to both open and closed strings)
3) Stop fretted notes with the left-hand finger

Ex. 5-3   Stop Ring

All three methods will help you immensely with control and tone, and will also help you learn how to avoid click and buzz. Furthermore, they will improve accuracy in executing notes. You'll find that if you practice these exercises regularly, with all the variations, they will greatly improve your dexterity in both hands. For a more challenging variation on this exercise, stop the previous string from ringing *just after* you pluck the next note.

SHIFTING ACCENTS

The goal of Example 5-4, Shifting Accents, is to learn how to accent, or emphasize, notes effectively. The accented note is played at a volume level slightly higher than the other notes. All the other notes are played at equal volume. All accented notes in a passage should be raised above non-accented notes by the same degree.

Ex. 5-4   Shifting Accents

Cumulative Accent with Stops (Example 5-5) is a variation Shifting Accents, involving right-hand string stops in measures 21 and 32. Additionally, you may want to go back to the exercise in Chapter 4 (Example 4-1). Instead of repeating each phrase in Dynamics once, repeat eight times, accenting each consecutive note of the phrase in sequence until all notes have been accented once.

Accents can be executed using either the free stroke or the rest stroke. Try employing both methods when playing the examples.

Ex. 5-5   Cumulative Accent with Stops

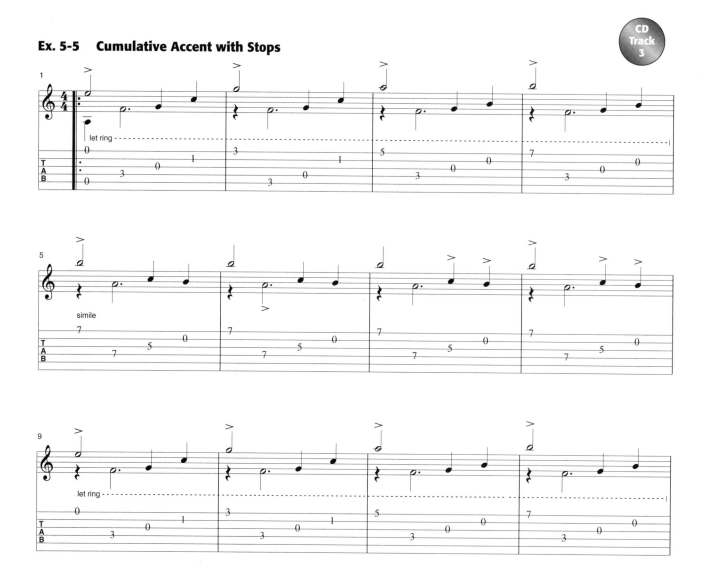

example continues...

Ex. 5-5 continued

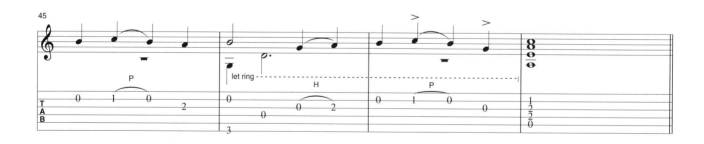

CHAPTER 6:

HAMMER-ONS AND PULL-OFFS

Learning to use hammer-ons and pull-offs effectively will help you be more articulate with a melody. Because both techniques soften the attack of a note, they are helpful in infusing your lines with a more vocal quality. They are also useful in sharpening the acumen of your fretting hand, since neither employs the picking hand.

A hammer-on is an application of energy onto the string—easy enough, though you have to remember to hammer on with enough force to generate a solid sound. The pull-off requires a bit more explanation and attention. Since there is no right-hand attack, you actually use the left-hand pull-off finger to pluck the string, and then rest that finger on an adjacent string. "Pluck" by pulling directly down with your left-hand finger, and then rest the finger on the next string. Technically speaking, if you just release, all you are getting is a reverse hammer-on. This is a common mistake and doesn't really qualify as a technique since it's very ineffective. The sound you get from this is so soft it is drowned out by other notes plucked more forcefully.

Shagadelic (Example 6-1), which I also like to call "the 007 exercise," is a great way to practice hammer and pull techniques.

Ex. 6-1   Shagadelic

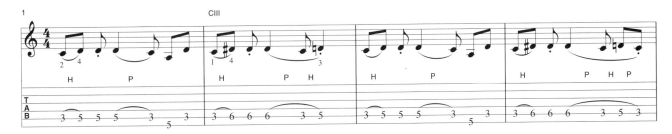

example continues...

Ex. 6-1 continued

For further practice with hammer-ons and pull-offs, use the lead line exercises in Building Fretboard Knowledge in Altered Tunings (Appendix). While ascending each scale, use hammer-ons for every second and fourth note played on the same string. When descending, play the second and fourth notes as pull-offs.

CHAPTER 7:

ALTERNATING RIGHT-HAND FINGERS

This chapter will help imprint right-hand finger alternation into the muscle memory. A basic principle for playing single-note parts underlies the exercises: *Avoid playing sequential notes on the same string with the same right-hand finger.* There are two good reasons to follow that principle: 1) It maximizes the economy of motion, making it easier to execute musical passages; and 2) It makes for a smoother delivery of an active melody.

The first two exercises offer two approaches for playing extended single-note lead lines and improvisations. Thumb-Index Alternating (Example 7-1) features the thumb-index alternation, which is notated with *pi pi* (thumb-index, thumb-index) or *ip ip*. Folk and jazz guitarists often use this technique, frequently in combination with a thumb pick.

Ex. 7-1 Thumb-Index Alternating

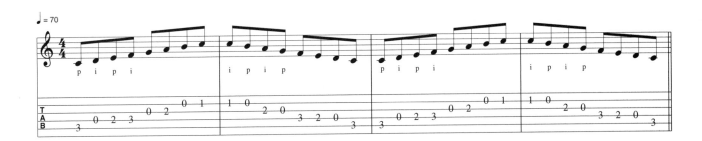

In First-Fingers Alternating #2 (Example 7-2), the index and middle fingers alternate and are notated as *im im* (index-middle, index-middle) or *mi mi*. Classical guitarists tend to use this technique. Most people find it is easier to achieve speed through thumb-index alternation, while first-fingers alternation is often prized for its roundness of tone.

Ex. 7-2   First-Fingers Alternating #2

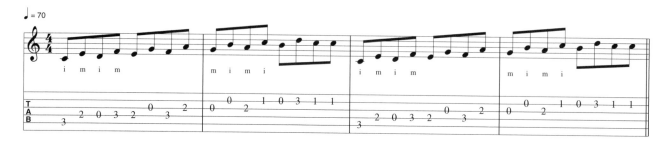

Alternating Right-Hand Fingers (Example 7-3) shows how all the right-hand picking fingers can be used when multiple strings are applied and the melody unfolds from arpeggiated phrases.

Ex. 7-3   Alternating Right-Hand Fingers

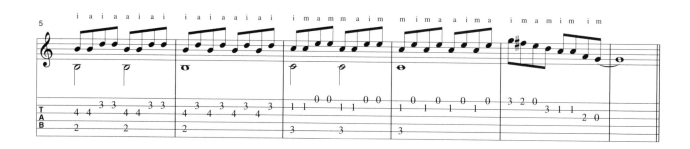

Practicing these exercises will help you develop an intuitive sense of how to attack single-note lead lines, and how to integrate melody easily and evenly into arpeggios.

As covered in Chapter 5, accenting can be used in arpeggiated phrases to bring out the melody. Learning how to alternate fingers effectively helps to smooth the contours of the melody. In solo guitar pieces, these two techniques are used in tandem with thumb-index alternation and first-fingers alternation for solo lead lines. Use the scale exercises in the Appendix, Building Fretboard Knowledge in Altered Tunings, for further practice.

CUMULATIVE EXERCISE: RIGHT-HAND PATTERN CHOICES

Example 7-4 draws its inspiration from the Gershwin tune "Summertime" and demonstrates the differences in right-hand fingering choices.

The first measure uses a typical folk-music finger pattern: *p i m*. Thereafter, the phrase repeats using a finger pattern more typical to classical guitar: *p i m a* (see measure 9). The difference between the two patterns lies in the use of the ring (*a*) finger. The approach to the bass is the same in both patterns, but in *p i m a* the ring finger is added.

Compare the sound of the two patterns using the *Am* chord as shown in measures 1 and 9. You may notice the bass in *p i m* comes out stronger and the melody is a little sharper. This is because only three fingers are in use. In *p i m a*, the sound is a little more balanced across all the strings, because the same amount of strength is more evenly distributed among four fingers than among three. You can probably get the two to sound nearly the same with a bit of work, but it's interesting to note the difference that naturally comes about.

In measures 3 and 4, two different patterns are used for the bass. In the 3rd measure, *p i m p* is used for the bass. In the 4th measure, *p p p p* is used for the bass. Can you hear the difference? It's an audible difference because the thumb is more dense and smaller than the index finger; the index finger is thinner, and has a sharper angle of attack. As a result, the bass comes out naturally thicker and louder than the melody.

There are several reasons why a player might choose one fingering pattern over another. First is convenience. In measure 9, *p i m a* comes in handy because we have an *A*-note as an inside voice—it's easier to use the index finger to hit that note because the index is already in position. Other reasons can be more subtle; for instance, the desire to have a sharper melody and more defined bass. Some may choose to use a pattern with more thumb strokes as a way of getting more low end into the arpeggio.

The *p i m* pattern is relatively easy, and as such is a crutch for many beginning players who have a hard time with *p i m a*. Many beginners are not inclined to use the ring finger, and instead plant it on the high *E* string or on the pickguard. As you can see from the exercises, it's probably a good idea to unlearn bad habits like these.

Our rendition also echoes the string-stop lessons from Chapter 5.

Ex. 7-4 Right-Hand Pattern Choices

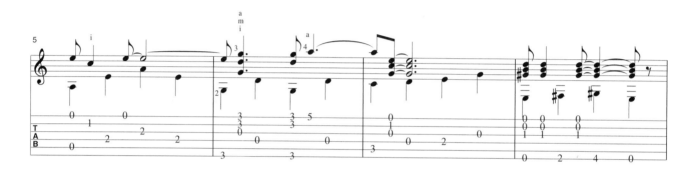

CUMULATIVE EXERCISE: MICHAEL'S THEME

In Michael's Theme (Example 7-5), many of the lessons we've covered are put to use, including varying color and dynamics; stopping notes; accenting; and alternating right-hand fingers.

This composition also contains some nifty chord shapes, some of which have been previewed in previous exercises. Because they use both open and fretted strings, they have the sound of chords from altered tunings despite the fact that the piece is in standard.

Play the accents as noted. Keeping a consistent *p i m a* pattern (*p* for the bass strings and *i m a* for the top three strings), the accent will shift among the outer and inner voices embedded in each arpeggio. Accenting serves a dual role by varying texture in the arpeggios and bringing out the melody. The melody is played a bit louder within the arpeggios, as noted.

In order to get the feel of the slight differences between rest strokes and free strokes, play the accenting in any phrase first as a rest stroke, then as a free stroke. You may discover that one way is more comfortable than another, or that a mix of rest stroke and free stroke works best for you. You may also find it easier to do a rest stroke with one finger in particular, such as the ring finger. If this is the case, use the exercises in previous chapters to achieve a balance in your ability to execute the rest stroke with all fingers.

String stopping (with the right and the left hand) is employed in the introductory phrases of this piece. You'll also notice that a thumb slap appears. See Chapter 9 for more about thumb slaps.

Michael's Theme will help you incorporate changes in volume, color, and accenting into your playing, and sharpen your ability with right- and left-hand string stopping. Enjoy!

Ex. 7-5 **Michael's Theme**

*Stop strings w/palm.

example continues...

Ex. 7-5 continued

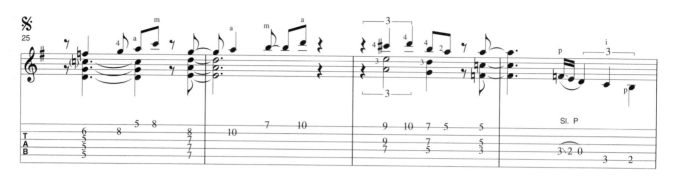

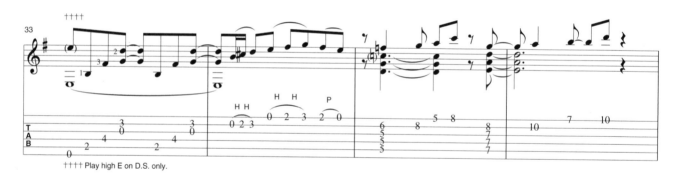

†††† Play high E on D.S. only.

example continues...

Ex. 7-5 continued

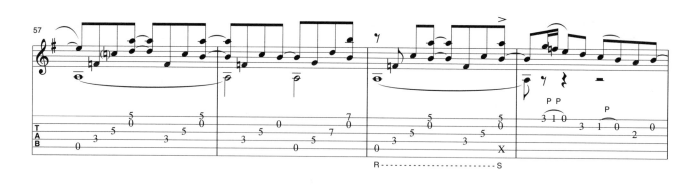

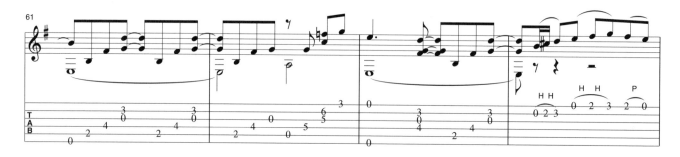

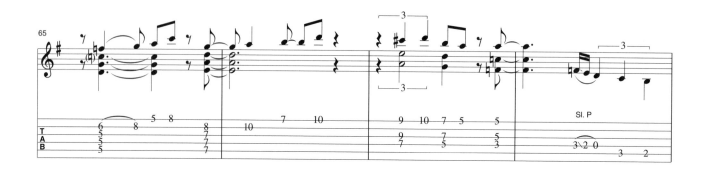

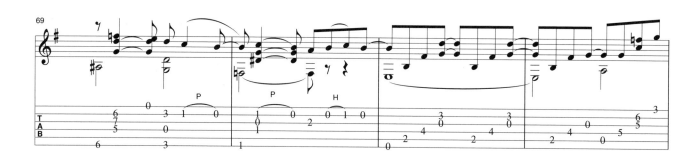

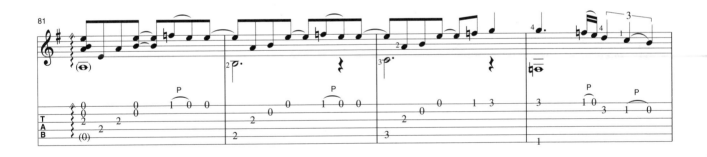

example continues...

Ex. 7-5 continued

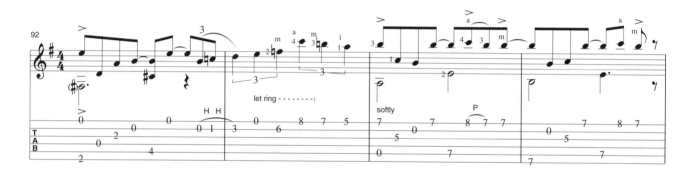

Coda

CHAPTER 8

HARMONIC CONVERGENCE

Harmonic notes are chiming, bell-like tones produced by plucking strings while a finger is placed lightly on the string. The easiest harmonics to produce are the "natural harmonics" occurring at the 3rd, 4th, 5th, 7th, 9th, 12th, 16th, and 19th frets. When producing harmonics, don't place your left-hand finger between the frets but instead play directly over the fretwire. There are two ways to produce natural harmonics:

Place the left hand on the string lightly—without pressing hard enough to fret a note—at a harmonic fret position, and pluck the string in a normal fashion with the right hand.

Place the tip of the right-hand index finger on the string lightly at a harmonic fret position. Pluck the string with the thumb, middle, or ring finger of the same hand. Harmonics produced by this technique are called "pluck harmonics."

Pluck harmonics can also be used to generate "artificial harmonics." Whereas no notes are fretted to produce natural harmonics, artificial harmonics are created by fretting a note with the left hand and then applying the index finger of the right hand one octave higher (12 frets up) on the same string. For example, fret a *G* on the 3rd fret of the 6th string. Now place the index finger of your right hand over the *G* at the 15th fret of the same string, and pluck with the thumb or ring finger.

You may find that it is more comfortable to pluck an artificial harmonic with the thumb or the ring finger, or even with the middle finger. Regardless of the comfort factor, learning a variety of methods will always open more possibilities. Using the ring finger is the most common technique among classical players. It comes in handy because it frees up the thumb and index finger for additional plucking.

Harmonic Play (Example 8-1) uses natural harmonics exclusively. Try both methods of achieving harmonics, and try to use different right-hand fingers when employing pluck harmonics.

Ex. 8-1   Harmonic Play

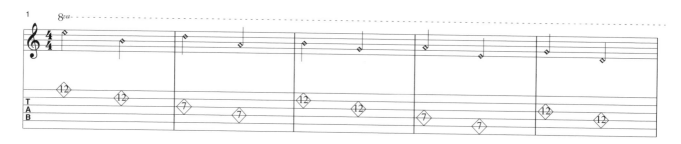

Artificial, Naturally (Example 8-2) combines natural and artificial harmonics, but *all are played as pluck harmonics*. To represent pluck harmonics in tablature, the first number, which is in a diamond, shows the fretting position; the second number, in parentheses, shows where the right-hand index finger rests.

Ex. 8-2   Artificial, Naturally

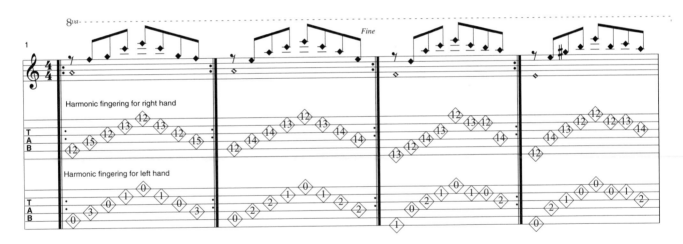

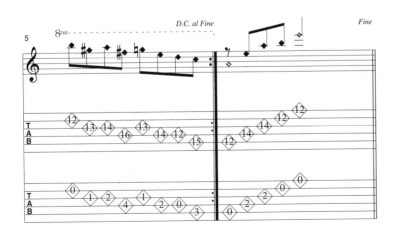

EXTENDED TECHNIQUE: HARMONIC SLAP

Generating a harmonic slap requires using the right hand to initiate harmonic sounds by "slapping" at harmonic positions on the fretboard. There are several ways to do this, and methods vary by what suits the player and the musical context.

The tactical approach for the right-hand slaps is to:

Slap lightly on the harmonic position (frets 12 and 19 are common frets for this kind of work)

Leave the right-hand finger on the fret position for a slight duration

Release

Depending on the context, players may slap with one, two, or even three fingers. Some are more comfortable "crossing" the middle finger over the index finger, as if to strengthen it, and then slapping. Others prefer using the index finger only. It's also possible to use just the middle finger, or to cross the index finger over the middle.

In fingerstyle guitar, it's common to hammer on the lower three strings with the left hand while slapping harmonics on the upper three strings with the right. This is exemplified in Exercise 8-3, Harmonic Slap #1.

Ex. 8-3   Harmonic Slap #1

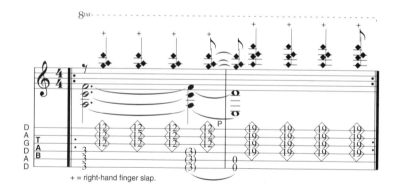

+ = right-hand finger slap.

Another possibility would be to use slap harmonics on the lower three strings while working sequences of hammer-ons and pull-offs in the upper four strings, as shown in Exercise 8-4, Harmonic Slap #2.

Ex. 8-4   Harmonic Slap #2

As a strategy for mastering this technique, try working the harmonic technique separately, first with the three treble notes, then with the three bass notes. Make sure you're getting equal volume and that you are achieving harmonics on just three strings. Experiment with how lightly you can slap and still get rich harmonics. Notice that if you slap down hard enough to hit the fretboard with your right-hand fingers, you'll get a percussive tapping sound. (That's not bad—in fact, it's a frequently used effect. However, it's not part of our exercises.)

After you've mastered the art of slapping at the 12th and 9th frets, practice just the hammer-ons and pull-offs. Hammer on, then pull off by moving back and down with enough force to approximate a pull-off sound with just the left hand. When you've achieved a rich, full sound, put the two "voices" together. Make sure you can really hear the hammer-ons, the pull-offs, and the harmonics.

CHAPTER 9:

PYRO-TECHNIQUES

Pyro-techniques is a colorful way to name several extended techniques. Slapping, tapping, and harmonics, in tandem with hammer-ons, pull-offs, and various percussive techniques, are the main elements of pyro-techniques. A more pervasive and fundamental technique is the thumb slap. On venturing into pyro-techniques, it's important not to become a "pyromaniac." A little taste of these techniques goes a long way both in composition and performance.

THUMB SLAP

The thumb slap is a simple percussive device that adds character and groove to a performance. The technique is simple: Slap your right-hand thumb down like a hammer onto the lowest string. If you are not using a thumb pick, hit the string with the flesh along the side of the nail. Players who do use a thumb pick will have to experiment with getting the pick out of the way by fitting it between or above the strings.

When you do it right, the string slaps down on the neck, rendering a sound that is comparable to a snare drum. In Example 9-1, Thumb Slap, the technique is used to create that snare drum sound on the upbeat (one *and* two *and*…). The first four measures should give you the idea. Attack the bass note as if it were a full quarter note, and then execute the thumb slap on the upbeat. Then add the melody, maintaining good time with the off-beat slaps.

The thumb slap is one of the most often used and one of the most effective percussion techniques on the guitar. In time you will find it natural to extend the idea into other forms of percussion. It may seem hard at first, but once you can do a good thumb slap, other devices will be easier to assimilate.

Ex. 9-1   **Thumb Slap**

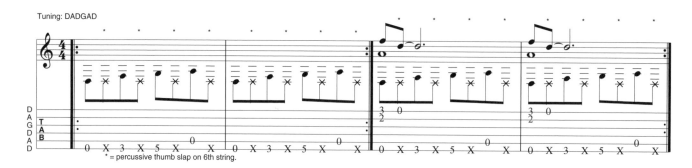

* = percussive thumb slap on 6th string.

BODY PERCUSSION

As you can see now, guitar is a percussive instrument. We have *string percussion*, such as the thumb slap, but we also have *body percussion*.

The body of the guitar is like a drum. Different tones and timbres are generated depending on where you thump the guitar: on the side, on the top, on the face of the upper front bout, on the face of the lower rear bout. There is also a difference in sound depending on whether or not fingernails are used in executing the hit.

Spend a few minutes checking this out on your own. Be careful not to thump too loud or hit too hard with your nails on the body—you can damage the guitar! Be aware that body percussion can produce spikes in volume, and could cause trouble for the soundman when you perform amplified (too much volume here will cause microphones to clip). You don't need to thump hard to get a solid sound.

Percussion (Example 9-2) extends the idea developed in Thumb Slap to include a "nail tap" on the upper left-hand bout of the guitar (above the neck, around fret 19), and a triplet with *a-m-i* followed by a "thumb-thump" (diagonally across, on the lower bout).

First practice the percussive motif as an isolated part. On the upbeat, practice tapping with the right-hand nail of *i*, on the bout above the 19th fret. Then practice alternating the nail tap with two thumb-thumps diagonally across, at the lower bout, on the next upbeat. The thumb-thump is achieved by tapping on the bout using the fleshy side of the thumb. Combine the single thumb-thump with a triplet formed by drumming with the fleshy part of the *a-m-i* fingers on the final upbeat. You know you've got it right when all percussive elements working in tandem sound like a cymbal (nail tap), foot-pedal drum, and bass drum.

Once you've got the hang of moving the arm from the front bout to the back bout, and the contrast of tap and thump, insert the melody and bass on the downbeat. What you then have is a simple melody, with bass, supported by a mini drum set.

Ex. 9-2   Percussion

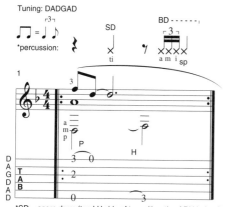

*SD = snare drum (tap LH side of top w/ti — tip of RH index finger)

BD = bass drum (tap on bottom RH side of top w/sp — side of thumb and a m i).

LEFT- AND RIGHT-HAND FRETWORK

Extended techniques often involve several different techniques working in conjunction. Example 9-3, Left- and Right-Hand Fretwork, introduces the basic technique of sequential pull-offs and hammer-ons with both the left and the right hands.

In the first three measures of this exercise, *the left hand only* is used to execute the descending cadence. Think of the sequence of hammer-ons and pull-offs as *pivot points* involving different finger combinations (first and third, second and third).

The second three measures introduce the *partial barre for the right hand.* Here, the progression is played by alternating between the second and third fingers of the left hand, with the index finger of the right hand executing the hammer-ons. In extended technique, the right-hand index finger is often used to generate power-chord-type sounds in the lowest strings. While the technique is inspiring visually, use it only when it's necessary to keep the left hand in its current position. For example, if the chord you want to play on the bass strings is in the third position, and you are playing with your left hand primarily in first and second, you may opt to use the partial right-hand barre).

The last four measures introduce the use of right-hand fretwork for inner voices and melody. In this sequence, the second and third fingers of the left hand alternate with fingers *i* and *m* to execute the passage.

The use of left-hand fingers to pluck open strings is presented in measures 2, 4, and 6 of this exercise as well. To pluck with the left-hand fingers, rest them on the strings indicated without using a hammer-on, and pull off lightly to generate the note values for the duration prescribed.

Ex. 9-3   Left- and Right-Hand Fretwork

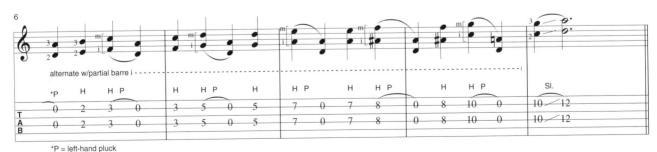

PUTTING IT ALL TOGETHER: FRETWORK WITH PERCUSSION

Example 9-4, Fretwork with Percussion, takes you to the final step by incorporating many of the pyro-techniques we've covered so far, including hammer-ons, pull-offs, harmonic slaps, and percussion.

This example, taken from the song "These Days" (see Example 9-6 below for the entire piece), illustrates how extended techniques typically work in tandem with one another. It represents a very simple concept: that extended technique should always be used to support musical content. Once one sees how easy left- and right-hand fret work, slapping, and tapping can be, it's easy to let these techniques dominate a composition. Instead of letting such devices drive my writing, though, I always try to use technique to support clear musical ideas, especially the melody.

Ex. 9-4   Fretwork with Percussion

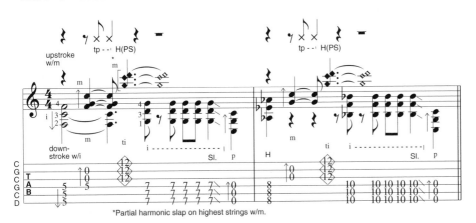

*Partial harmonic slap on highest strings w/m.

CUMULATIVE EXERCISES: "DEE DUM," "THESE DAYS," AND "DUTCH CRUNCH"

The three musical examples that follow will help you learn a bit more about how extended techniques are put into the context of fingerstyle guitar compositions. These tunes essentially extend the ideas covered to this point into full-blown compositions.

All three are in alternate tunings. "Dee Dum" is written in *DADGAD*, and "These Days" is in *CGCGCD*. Both of these tunings are now considered conventional in fingerstyle guitar. The final composition, "Dutch Crunch," is written in a more unusual tuning: *CG#D#GCD#*.

Percussion is occasionally used in these tunes.

Again, be careful not to thump or tap too hard. You don't need to damage your guitar to use the techniques effectively.

A few brief notes to get you on your way:

Dee Dum (Example 9-5)

In this composition, the thumb slap is used along with percussion as a motif. The slaps, heard on upbeats, contrast with a very simple melodic phrase. Left-hand fret work (with no right-hand attack) is used for the melody.

These Days (Example 9-6)

Similar strategies are used in this example, but the composition is more complex in terms of structure and melody. This song also employs harmonic slaps with percussion, but again only as a motif for representing an idea that's important to the song's structure.

Dutch Crunch (Example 9-7)

This example provides the most extensive use of extended technique, including hammer-ons and pull-offs, harmonics, and thumb slaps. Despite the complexity of the piece, you'll note that no technique is ever employed without a clear motif or melody in mind. They are all essential to the structure and flow of the composition.

Technique doesn't drive composition—ideas and emotive content do.

Ex. 9-5   Dee Dum

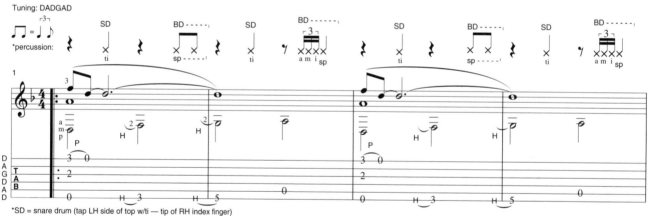

*SD = snare drum (tap LH side of top w/ti — tip of RH index finger)

BD = bass drum (tap on bottom RH side of top w/sp — side of thumb and a m i).

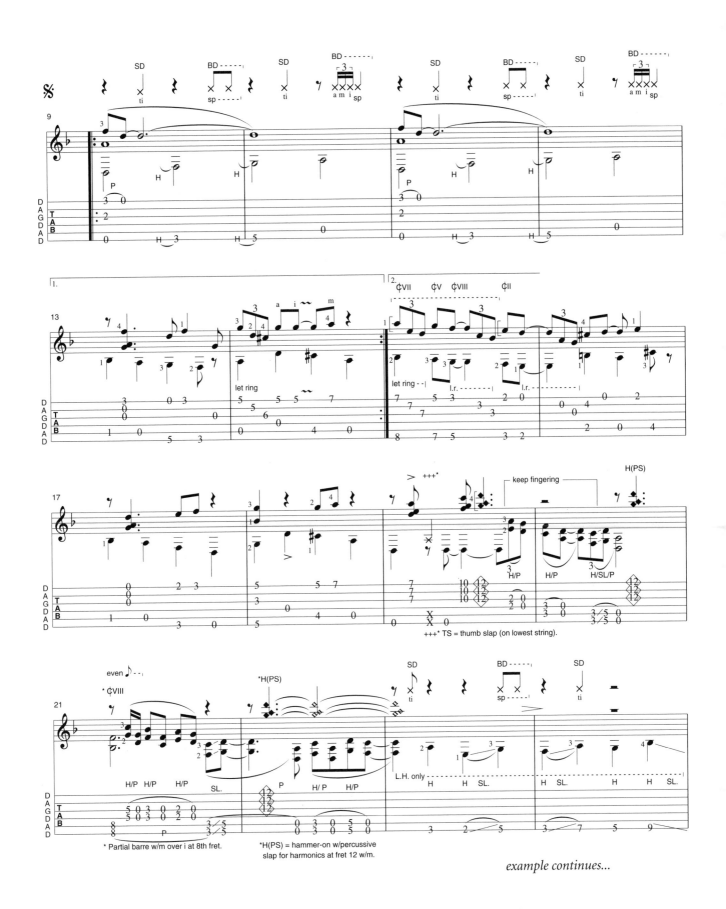

+++* TS = thumb slap (on lowest string).

* Partial barre w/m over i at 8th fret.

*H(PS) = hammer-on w/percussive
slap for harmonics at fret 12 w/m.

example continues...

Ex. 9-5 continued

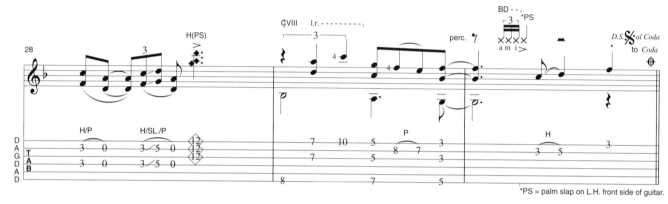

*PS = palm slap on L.H. front side of guitar.

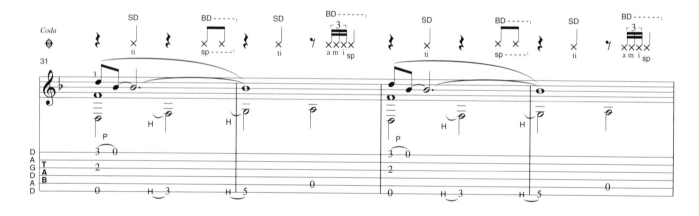

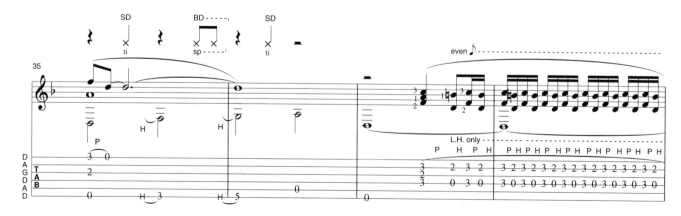

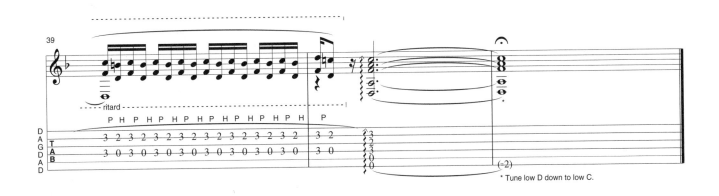

* Tune low D down to low C.

Ex. 9-6   **These Days**

example continues...

Ex. 9-6 continued

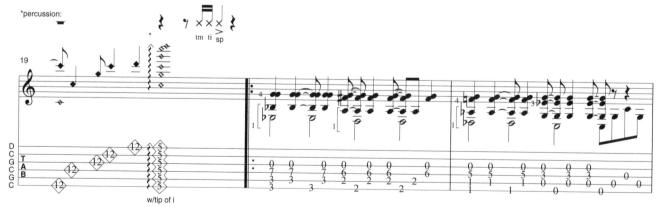

*Percussion on guitar top above fret 19 using nail on m & i and side of thumb.

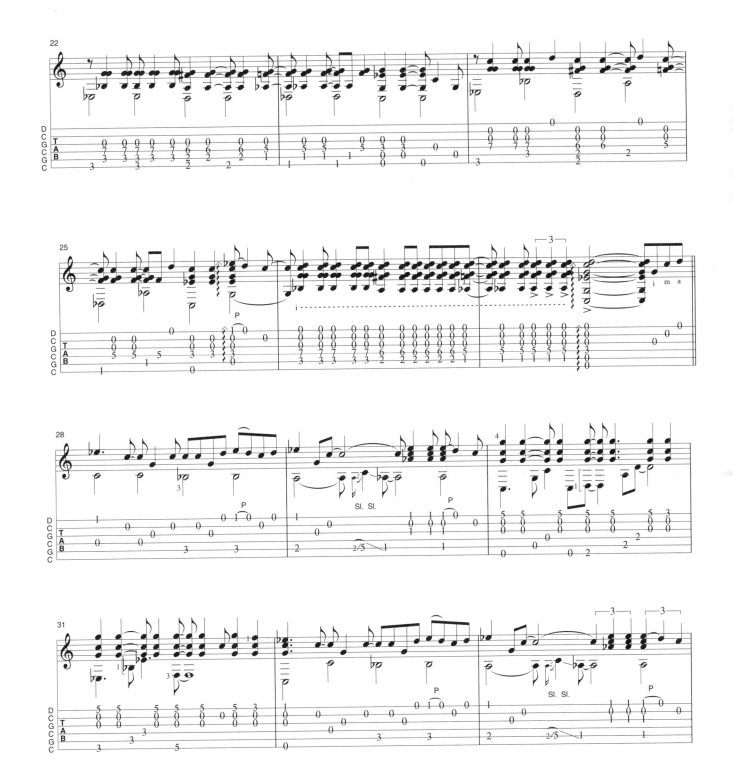

example continues...

Ex. 9-6 continued

*Partial harmonic slap on highest strings w/m.

tp = percussion w/tip of thumb on guitar top above fret 16.

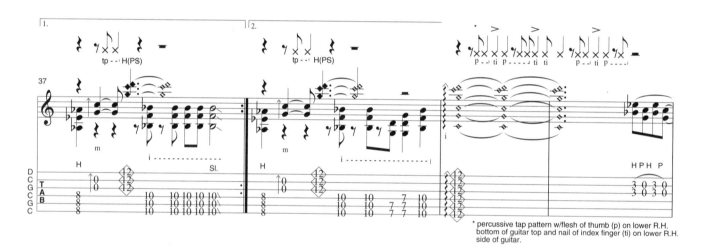

* percussive tap pattern w/flesh of thumb (p) on lower R.H.
bottom of guitar top and nail of index finger (ti) on lower R.H.
side of guitar.

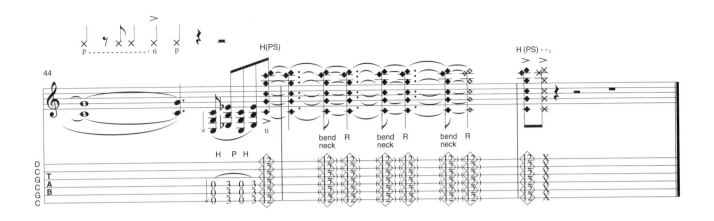

Ex. 9-7 Dutch Crunch

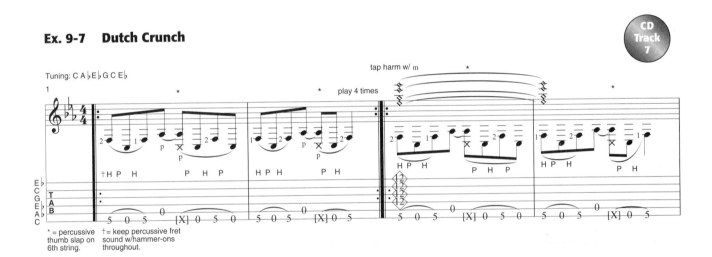

* = percussive thumb slap on 6th string.

† = keep percussive fret sound w/hammer-ons throughout.

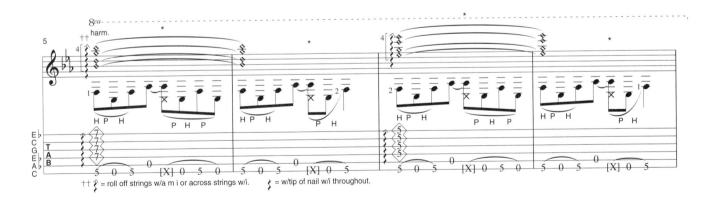

†† ⌃ = roll off strings w/a m i or across strings w/i.   ⌃ = w/tip of nail w/i throughout.

example continues...

Ex. 9-7 continued

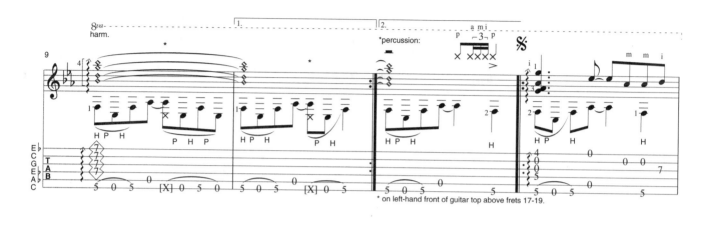

* on left-hand front of guitar top above frets 17-19.

††† Staccato mark (•) indicates RH string stop.

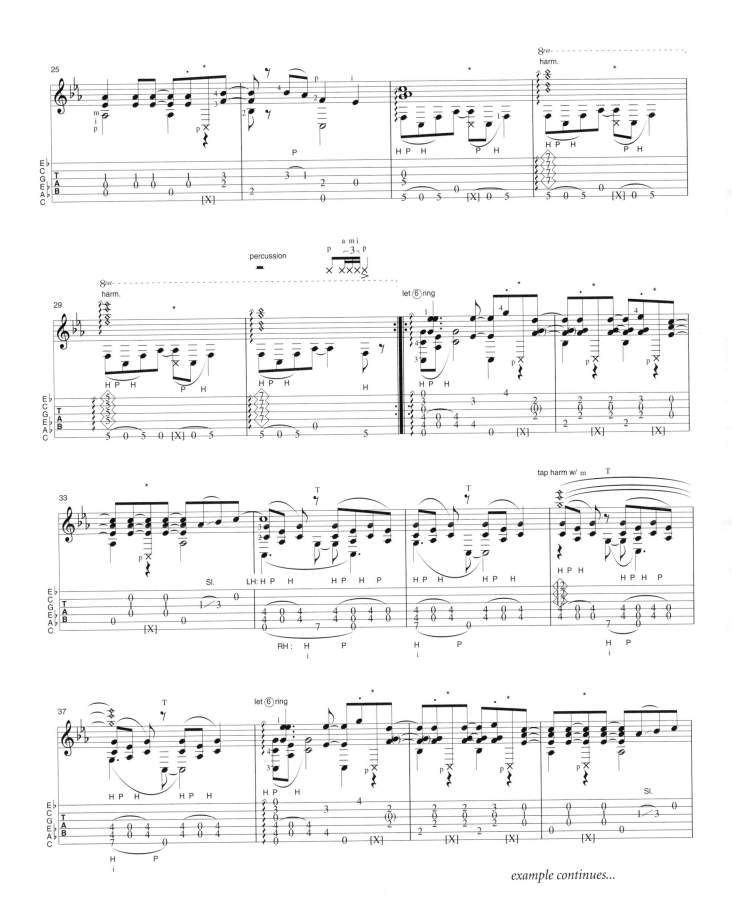

example continues...

Ex. 9-7 continued

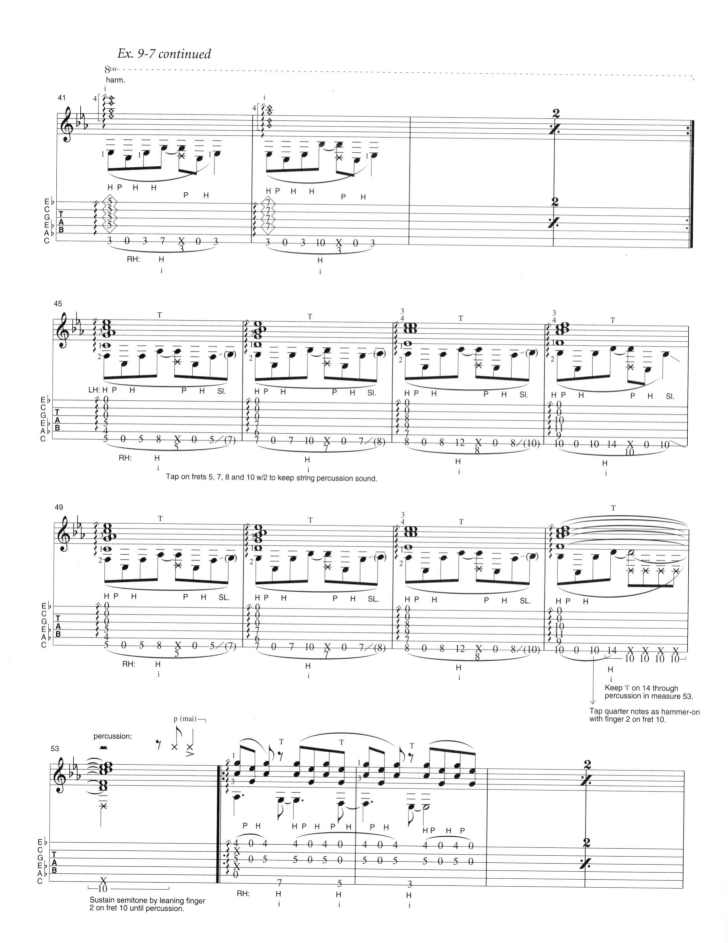

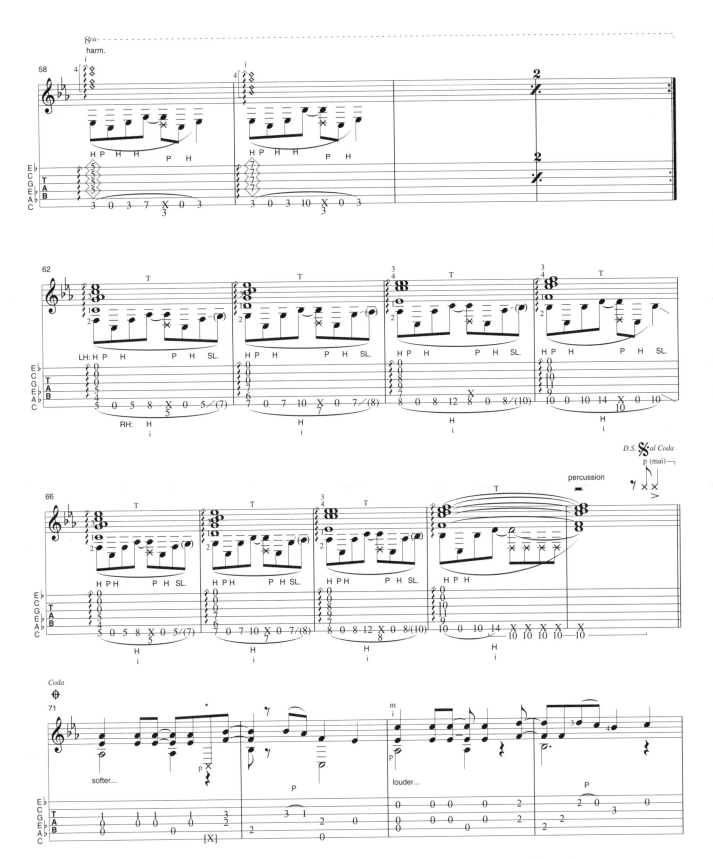

example continues...

Ex. 9-7 continued

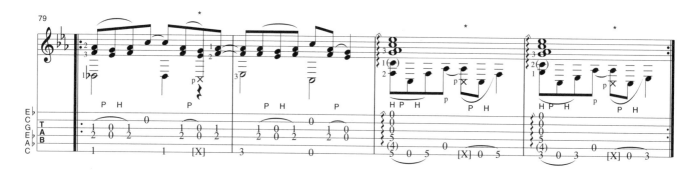

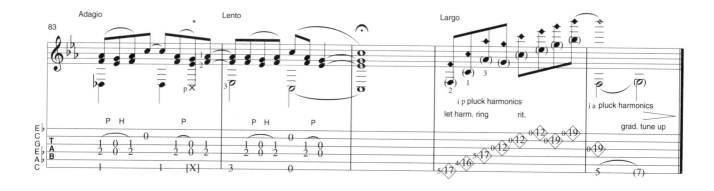

CHAPTER 10:
COMPOSITION AND CREATIVITY

"It is not my *music. It is* the *music. And I am a servant of it."*

—Pierre Bensusan

I'd like to begin this chapter on composition with a few words from Peppino D'Agostino.

> The polyphonic nature of the guitar is perfectly served by using multiple fingers of the right hand. Similar to an orchestra, which needs multiple instruments to fully express its potential, the guitar reaches its best when its harmonic texture, contrapuntal lines, and distinctive melodic voices are conjuring together toward beauty.
>
> The steel-string guitar, with its voice similar at times to a harpsichord, offers a very distinctive timbre and sonority which are very unique and soulful. The opportunity to use a palette of sound effects such as string bending, percussive and slide techniques, complex open tunings, or bent harmonics makes the steel-string guitar a real favorite instrument of choice.
>
> The challenges in composing for steel-string guitar are multiple and perhaps difficult to overcome. The general tendency is to either relax into predictable and boring musical grounds or to showcase useless displays of speed. The most talented steel-string composers are the ones that are able to create beautiful melodies supported by intelligent harmonies and powerful grooves. The steel-string guitar should be approached as an orchestra with infinite possibilities.

The main opportunity composing in guitar provides is the ability to layer multiple voices in tandem, to support a coherent idea replete with emotive content. A composer is like a story-teller who uses technique as his or her narrative craft. The main challenge in composing on guitar lies in learning to use technique to support the portrayal of musical ideas, and to communicate emotion. To do this effectively, you have to learn how to separate the "song" from the guitar. It's always good to ask yourself *what would the song sound like if it weren't played on the guitar.* If it can't stand on its own, *as a song*, that someone could sing, or an orchestra could play, you likely don't have a truly memorable piece.

Learning to separate the process of composing from your explorations on the fretboard is crucial here. The compositional process should inspire you to develop your technique, in order to support it. If you find an interesting technical idea, incorporate it into a theme in the piece, or into a motif. You may find you develop many more interesting techniques and ideas than can be incorporated in the piece. That's okay. You don't have to include *everything* that emerges out of the process of generating musical ideas. The most appropriate approach is to employ just what is necessary to convey the main ideas and feelings, making the determination on intuition in conjunction with the analytic tools provided in this chapter. You can save the rest as "nuggets" for future ideas.

SEPARATING VOICES: IDENTIFYING BASS, RHYTHM, AND MELODY

Composing on acoustic guitar involves the consistent use of melody, harmony, and accompaniment. In a well-composed piece, these elements interact as distinct voices working together towards a shared musical goal. *Separating the voices* is a simple technique you can use to identify each of the individual voices.

In creating songs for guitar, the ability to distinguish between the melody (lead voice), the rhythm accompaniment (chordal or harmonic voices), and the bass (the bass line foundation) is crucial. As an exercise in distinguishing among the three parts, see Example 10-1a, "These Days" Intro in 3 Voices. Compare this example to the intro to "These Days" as originally written, Example 10-1b.

Ex. 10-1a These Days, Intro

Ex. 10-1b

Knowing how to identify and develop these separate parts can help in several significant ways:

Troubleshooting. If you are having trouble playing a particular phrase or part of a phrase, you'll want to isolate and analyze the part so that you can practice it more effectively.

Accuracy. It's a common error to hold notes shorter or longer than their appropriate duration, often due to technical challenges or to working strictly on a "kinetic level"; that is, with what fits nicely under the fingers rather than what is prescribed by the written part. Separating the voices can help you see where you may need to hold a note for a shorter or longer duration to achieve the correct sustain. It can also help you determine whether you are actually playing the right notes. Sometimes a player will even miss notes entirely, especially in the bass and accompaniment parts.

DEVELOPING COMPLETE PARTS

When composing, the original seed of the idea is often formed only partially. You may have one piece of a good melody line, arpeggiated chord sequence, or nifty rhythmic motif, but any of the three may be underdeveloped. Separating the voices helps you see which of the parts you need to work on in order to develop your idea completely.

Melody Note Choice. Separating the voices is especially helpful with the development of a melody. Separating the voices helps "free" melody for further development up or down the fretboard. If you base your melody strictly on what works well "kinetically"—that is, on what falls nicely under the fingers—you may be limiting the range of the melody to what's easily reached within a small range (say, four frets) of the seminal idea. Looking at the melody separately will help you open up its potential for variation. For example, after repeating the same melodic idea twice in These Days (see Chapter 9, Example 9-6), I *vary* it in the second section by jumping up an octave (measure 10) in a phrase that eventually descends back down to the octave of the first phrase. Building ideas like this into a song requires exploring where the melody might go if it were extended beyond the first position on the guitar. Temporarily freeing the melody from the other parts may shine some light on such possibilities.

Melody Articulation. Separating parts can also free you up to explore choices in articulation. Examples 10-2 (Articulating with Plucks) and 10-3 (Articulating with Slides) illustrate how the melody from Example 7-4 (Chapter 7) could be varied slightly. In Example 10-2, the melody on strings 2 and 1 falls easily into place. In Example 10-3, a pull-off is added, as are slides on strings 2 and 3. Notice when playing these examples that the quality of the melody is made smoother by adding the pull-off and that the timbre of the melody changes when it is played on the lower strings. Freeing the melody from the other parts can help you see how it may sound in other fretboard contexts.

Ex. 10-2 Summer Theme

Ex. 10-3 Summer Theme

Bass and Accompaniment. When bass and rhythm parts are separated from the melody, the patterns in those parts often emerge. Once a pattern is identified, it's easier to maintain the part and play it consistently. For example, in These Days, the introductory melody is supported with an alternating bass line using open or easy-to-reach fretted notes in the first position. You'll notice that the alternating bass pattern is maintained as much as possible through the third and second positions of the descending cadence (measures 10–13). Additionally, the accompaniment pattern is kept as consistent as possible with the introductory phrase as well.

SINGING AND HEARING YOUR MUSIC

Learning to separate the voices doesn't require vast harmonic knowledge or the ability to notate. It demands a much more essential and difficult skill: *hearing* the music you are making. You need to be able to *hear* the music even when you are not *playing* it on guitar. One of the best ways to accomplish this is through singing. If you want your guitar to sing, you have to start singing yourself.

Learn to sing each part in a piece separately: phrase by phrase, section by section, and then in its entirety. Just sing the melody first. Then, sing the bass. Finally, sing just the accompaniment (usually, this is the toughest skill to develop).

After that, try to learn the skills of "hearing in your imagination." In your mind's ear, *hear* the bass and accompaniment together. Learn how to sing the melody while hearing possible bass and accompaniment patterns to support the melody, and vice versa. Finally, learn to hear it all together.

Using a metronome in tandem with your singing can prove indispensable. You can also try "visualizing" yourself playing each part and the section you are working on—that is, imagining yourself playing—while you are singing. Undertaking this process will help you build confidence and reinforce your visual and aural memory of the piece while also helping you grow into the music.

LEADING WITH THE MELODY IN COMPOSITION

There are a wide variety of compositional techniques, but it's best to *lead with the melody*. This is especially true when you are first trying your hand at composing. Using this approach, the bass and accompaniment play supporting roles in the arrangement you create for the melody. If you fully develop the lead line, the chord changes can fall naturally; or at least, the possibilities are easier to identify. As the melody changes, the chords will change with them.

If you have a solid, well-developed melody, all you have to do is make sure that the bass and accompaniment patterns you choose are well thought out and consistent. If you choose to vary them, do so in a manner that supports the overall coherence of the composition. A simple example of this can be found again in These Days, where the key changes from *C* major to *C* minor. In measures 28–29, the melody and the bass are approached very similarly to the way they're handled in the intro phrase, with only slight variations.

IDENTIFYING STRUCTURE

Writing a song on acoustic guitar is kind of like writing a poem. The song consists of different phrases with distinct sections, which, I believe, are similar to stanzas in poetry. To apply some common methodology to your composing, designate sections and phrases with letters.

The typical "lyrical" folk song usually has an ABA(C)A structure ("C" is the optional bridge). Instrumental fingerstyle guitar songs are usually more intricate in structure but do have a symmetry involving repetition of simple themes with variations. Also, a *coda*—a finale or final statement drawing the piece to a conclusion—is very common.

It's really up to you what to denote as a "section." But, new sections are typically signified by departures in harmony, melody, or rhythm.

The following chart illustrates the structure of These Days (Chapter 9, Example 9-6).

Structure of These Days: AA B(B1) C D(D1) E

A:	Introductory Theme: major melody	measures 1–9
B:	Variation I: first ending	measures 10–14
B1:	Variation I: second ending	measures 10–13, then 15–19
C:	Short "Baden Powellish" motif	measures 20–27
D:	Variation II: minor percussive melody; first ending	measures 28–37
D1:	Variation II: minor percussive melody; second ending	measures 28–36, then 38
E:	Ending: Coda; rhythmic and percussive motif	measures 39–end

As you can see, the piece consists of an introductory theme, repeated twice, and two variations, each with different endings. The "Baden Powellish" motif is inserted as a "break" or "mini-interlude" between variations. The piece also includes an ending, or coda.

REPETITION, VARIATION, AND THE CREATIVE PROCESS

Variation and repetition influence the development and structure of a composition. They are really quite simple ideas. To see how it works, try the "airplane music" experiment. The next time you're in an airplane, analyze one of the songs they pipe in before takeoff. You can do the same experiment listening to the music that's piped in to stores, elevators, etc. The songs are very simple, so this will be "easy listening" for you. Listen for the "main theme" and the "subthemes," or variations, in the melody. Try to figure out the chord changes that "pilot" the piece, and what kinds of rhythmic ideas are included to help make the piece "fly." This same simple analysis you apply to Kenny G or John Tesh in the preflight program is the same one you can use in your own creative process—albeit, hopefully, with results that are more personally satisfying to you.

Variation and repetition are very intuitive, and you don't need to be a rocket scientist to figure *that* out. The goal is to write a piece that makes well-balanced use of repetition and variation. Let intuition and feeling guide you, and learn how to become your own judge.

There are rules, but none is hard and fast. Great songs usually have one or two really interesting main ideas, repeated—perhaps with minor variations—to maximize their impact, and supported with subordinate ideas that provide contrast to main ones. If you are not using a "lyrical" song structure—that is, verse/chorus/bridge—you're probably going to need a coda at some point. Believe it or not, that's about it.

Variation and repetition are at play at every layer in the musical strata—in the structure, themes, and phrases. Harmony, melody, and rhythm are the "landing strips" for variation and repetition. You already have the ability to understand variation and repetition in compositions, regardless of your formal training or skill level. You have spent a lifetime listening to music, and as a result you have a whole "library" of sounds in your head and heart to choose from. Cultivating a sense of the particulars about what you like and why will help you turn this aural lexicon into your own musical palette. The more active you become at listening for the balance of variation and repetition in familiar music, the more you will be able to turn that knowledge into a tool for your own creative voice.

Start with music you are working with now. If you have a good melodic idea in a composition but want to extend or rework it, you can try altering the harmony, rhythm, or parts of the melody. If you have a great harmony but no melody, you can experiment with different melodies that may fit with the harmony. Likewise, if you have a great rhythmic idea, you can try placing it in different melodic and harmonic contexts. A well-balanced composition is achieved by ensuring that all the domains of music—harmony, melody, and rhythm—are taken fully into consideration and fully support the content that you are portraying. So the more knowledge you build in each domain, the more capable you will become.

ITERATION, PROGRESSION, AND SEQUENTIAL STRUCTURING

The structure and flow of compositions are influenced by the processes that form them. Three main processes underlie most fingerstyle compositions—iteration, progression, and sequential structuring. The more you build your technical knowledge, the more you can use them as creative tools. But even if you work intuitively, one or all of these processes will be involved in the creation of your work. A piece's flow naturally reflects where you're at developmentally as a composer and what your musical tastes and values are.

Iteration is a process of repetition and replacement as a central idea is repeated, some elements are replaced while others are retained. This is a great way to extend melodies, since you can keep hammering the listener with the melody's "nuggets" by repeating them over and over. But because there is constant variation in at least some part of the melody over a phrase or section, your listeners won't get bored.

Progression commonly refers to the way in which the piece "progresses" harmonically. If there is a chord change, you have a harmonic progression. Chord progressions usually happen naturally in the context of changes in the melody. Again, try the "airplane music" experiment: Listen to the way chord changes accompany a melody. When the chords change, a progression is happening. The rules governing harmonic progressions are culturally based, and there is no better place to capture the "musical pulse" of a culture than in its background music. The more time you spend as an active listener wherever you are, the easier it will be to identify common chord changes.

A song typically starts on the key's tonic chord (the "I" chord) and progresses from there. A typical chord progression is I–IV–V. Those Roman numerals signify the positions on the scale you are working in and the related chords. Obviously, the more you know about chord structure and harmony, the more versatile you will be at utilizing these tools more effectively. It's perfectly okay to work with the abilities you have and progress in your knowledge intuitively over time.

Sequential structuring is a modern concept in composition. Essentially, it involves putting together ideas that are not necessarily related harmonically, melodically, or rhythmically. In a sequential approach, the structure is defined by the sequence of loosely related musical phrases or themes you decide to compile into a composition, nothing more or less. The composition may not "progress" in accordance to the cultural tradition governing harmony. Or the melody may not "progress" in a manner intuitive to most ears. Whatever you want to do is okay. There are no rules. If this is the way you are feeling, perhaps the sequential route is the way to go. Sequential structuring can be found in the works of great artists like Stravinsky (*The Rite of Spring*) and John Cage. You can also hear influences of this thinking in the "free-form" jazz improvisation styles pioneered by artists like Herbie Hancock and Wayne Shorter. But the approach is not limited to modern composition and jazz. In fingerstyle guitar, artists like Alex deGrassi have spoken of a "stream of consciousness" approach to creating compositions. Sequential structuring can also be found in John Fahey's "American Primitive" work as well.

DO IT NOW

You don't need a master's degree in music or to have studied with a master composer in order to write music. You can start right now with the skills you have. Some of the world's best fingerstyle guitarists have had little to no formal training: as Don Ross says, "no gurus, no teachers." That said, the more you know, the more you grow. The more you create, the more motivated you will be to increase your technical understanding of guitar and music theory to support the process. It's true that almost all the great guitar composers have studied theory on their own in order to fully inhabit their compositional process and gain technical skill and confidence. If they can do it, there's no reason you can't.

Start by working with the skills you have and try to recognize the processes you are using to structure the piece. If you have a really great theme or phrase but feel like you need to have a chord change to take the composition into a new direction, then you are thinking on the level of harmonic progression. But if you come up with a new section that doesn't fit a "typical" harmonic progression and your intuition tells you that's right, stick with it. In this case, you may be thinking sequentially. If you have a good part of a melody and don't know what to do next, try iteration as a means of extending the melody—that just means you'll keep part of the original melodic idea while replacing another with something else.

Most musical processes happen naturally. Melody may be produced through an iterative process, for example. But we don't randomly generate melodies like a computer—it happens through the filter of our personalities and life experiences. Iteration is only a label that describes the process. Like life itself, music is a "self-guided" tour. It's not about theories, notes, or numbers—those are just means for describing the journey. The opportunities are boundless. But the more you learn to recognize what techniques you are using, the better off you'll be.

WRITE IT DOWN!

Even if you can't notate music, you can still label your sections with letters, numbers, or titles. Writing down the structure of a composition aids in its development by helping you recognize emerging patterns. For instance, if you have an A and B section of a piece under construction and don't know where to go next, you can try creating a C section or repeating A or B. If you like what you hear somewhat, but not enough, you can create a B1 or an A1; that is, a variation on one of the original sections. This process can also help you see if you've achieved a satisfying balance between repetition and variation. Even if you don't know what the chords are, you can still tell when they change, and make note of that. You can do the same thing with the melody and rhythm.

Writing it down is the best form of analysis. Start doing your own analysis now, creating labels for the different phrases and sections you are employing in the compositions you are creating. If you are not notating, slowly take the plunge into learning that skill. The great thing about modern notation programs such as Finale is the playback feature. Even if you can only enter chord changes into your notation program, you can still use the playback feature to see if you're getting the sounds you're going for. Don't feel blocked or inhibited by your perceived lack of knowledge or ability. Anyone can do this, if they want. We all have music in our hearts, so it's an illusion to think otherwise.

BACK TO THE MELODY

If this seems a bit baffling, just remember: Most memorable songs are formed around a great melody. So, it's important to always keep your energy centered on development and support of the melody. In melody, simple ideas with high emotion are the most effective, because they are the most memorable. Variation and repetition give life and support to the best parts of your melodic ideas. Repeat the best melodic ideas as often as possible—but not to the point of being redundant. If you vary those ideas too much, listeners may lose sight of that great melody at the core. So, you can see, it's a balancing act.

TECHNIQUE AND CREATIVITY

I'm suggesting that guitar composition is *poetic*. It's *lyrical* without necessarily using the typical song structures employed in music with actual lyrics. The lyrical quality is preserved by establishing melody as the primary focus of the composition. The poetic content narrates moods and images to convey a wordless message. The structure of the composition is defined by series of harmonically related phrases, like stanzas in poetry, using various creative developmental tools (iterative, sequential, progression). Balanced structure and effective functional use of repetition and variation, in support of a well-developed melody with clear themes, constitute the hallmarks of an effective composition.

VIRTUOSITY AND CONTENT

"You can build out your composition to portray the technical potential of the instrument."

—Laurence Juber

The composition in essence tells a story, and it's important to make sure that every feature of the composition supports that story. Because we are telling this story on a specific instrument, we have our technical palette and the technical potential of the guitar to use (and contend with) in communicating this story. What we choose to do with technique—variations in tone, timbre, volume, articulation—are influencing factors on the "narration."

Technique is part of the story for both audience and composer. In some cases this is a liability and in others an opportunity. Many guitarists want to make music that incorporates groundbreaking technique to illustrate the virtuosic potential of the instrument (and, in some cases, of themselves). Discerning guitar audiences want to see and hear innovative technical approaches in composition. So, composing for guitar presents the additional challenge of integrating technique into the creation and performance process.

But in the end, music played on the guitar isn't music *for the guitar*. And, it shouldn't be intended as music *just for guitarists*. It's music, for people, using guitar as its medium. So, the temptation to use guitar compositions as a forum to display virtuosity must be balanced with the use of technique in the service of communicating valuable musical content. With this balance, a composer/performer stands to reach a much broader audience.

THEMES VS. MOTIFS

The fingerstyle guitarists I love the most are clearly adept technically. Their technique is almost always applied in unapologetic support of the music. Because of this, the music, rather than technique, dominates the message conveyed. When virtuosity is a feature they choose to highlight, it's done in a way that augments rather than detracts from the musical content. The virtuosic elements are built into the composition in the form of motifs.

Take a moment to understand the distinction between themes and motifs.

- *Themes* are the primary "drivers" of a composition. They are fully developed melodic phrases integrating harmonic and rhythmic support. Themes can incorporate virtuosity, but they are indispensable to the overall message in the composition. The extended techniques integrated into themes act as support tools for the arrangement.

- *Motifs* are phrases highlighting rhythmic, harmonic, and/or brief melodic ideas. Motifs can be used as intros, hooks, embellishments, or interludes. In fingerstyle guitar, they often utilize innovative, virtuosic technique. They add contrastive elements to the overarching melody. Motifs are used to emphasize virtuosic ideas, but they are not the primary "drivers" of the composition.

The first three bars of Michael's Theme (Chapter 7, Example 7-5) represent an example of a harmonic motif, used as an introductory idea. It is essentially an arpeggiated chord, something found quite often in introductory segments of fingerstyle guitar compositions. The texture of the phrase is augmented through the inclusion of shifting accents. But you can see that, even with the addition of accent shifting, the phrase would quickly become redundant without the inclusion of a melody. So, this is an example of *a motif that evolves into a theme* through the gradual addition of a melody at measure 16. Without the addition of the melody, this nice little arpeggio goes nowhere.

The distinction between themes and motifs has helped me in my own strategies for addressing the challenge of balance between virtuosity and content. Use of motifs provides a forum for highlighting interesting technical ideas in a way that is supportive of the overall message and melodic content of compositions. But you can't go anywhere substantive in composition without strong, memorable, well-developed themes.

INTEGRATING EXTENDED TECHNIQUE

From the guitarist's perspective, harmonic slaps, right-hand fretwork, left-handed fretwork, and percussion are often seen as the "holy grails" of skillful playing. The perception is that players with facility in extended technique are on another level entirely, and that those who can't are only initiates into the inner circle. But, as the exercises I've created illustrate, they really aren't that difficult. If you can pat your head with one hand and rub your stomach with the other, while still chewing gum, odds are that you'll eventually be able to master the extended techniques with a little practice.

Mastering their application in composition, however, requires *effective integration* of extended technique into the context of bass, accompaniment, and melody. Extended technique should be used in the service of a cohesive musical statement, rather than as a replacement for one.

Dutch Crunch (Chapter 9, Example 9-7) represents what I mean by effective integration. In this piece, extended technique is used as a *lead in* to melody or as *support* of the melody, rather than as a *replacement for* melody. In the first two measures, the bass is introduced using left-hand fretwork, with the right hand used only for thumb slaps. This catchy intro groove is extended into a motif involving the use of slap harmonics (right-hand fretwork) in measures 9-11. This motif is augmented with percussion in thumb slaps throughout and simple taps on the body of the guitar concluding the section at measure 11.

Then, the melody is introduced in the main theme, keeping all the elements introduced through extended technique in the previous measures. Measure 34 introduces the technique of using the first right-hand finger to manage parts of the bass line, which is carried on throughout the second half of the piece in different sections. You'll notice that the addition of this technique was included because it's *necessary* for the implementation of the bass progression, not because it's technically interesting.

The words from that old blues song—"It ain't the meat, it's the motion"—apply to extended technique. It's not what you are capable of, technically, that defines your creative potential. Our skills are always growing. Instead, it's what you do with it that counts. This is why it's very important to develop effective methods of integrating extended technique into the compositional process, so that you can enhance the communication of your intended content.

The more you explore the potential of various techniques in each tuning, the more you'll be able to extend your fretboard knowledge into compositions. The application of extended technique should always be guided by the goal of developing cogent themes and memorable melodies. In fact, the process through which you learn to negotiate extended technique into your general style informs the *signature*—the unique aspect of your sound, recognizable as you—of your compositions and performance. The fact that you can, and must, tackle the process on your own is crucial, since it will help you in developing your creative voice.

SUMMARY

Fretboard knowledge, both in standard tuning and altered tuning, goes hand in hand with the development of creative potential. Altered tunings have certain "flavors" that make them interesting to explore, and each has a fretboard logic all its own. When you develop seeds of ideas in a new tuning, you can expand the potential of your music by learning the scales, arpeggios, and cadences compatible with these ideas.

Likewise, the ability to develop your own compositional and performing signature in altered tunings is enhanced by developing *your own palette of extended techniques*. Learn to see the technical parallels between different altered tunings you use, and even standard tuning. Learn to see where they overlap with one another.

Composing guitar music involves the *consistent use of melody, bass, and accompaniment*. The most intuitive approach to developing compositions is through leading with the melody line, viewing bass and accompaniment as the pillars of solo guitar arrangements.

Singing and *"hearing in the mind's ear"* are the most effective tools for analysis and practice. Develop the ability to separate each "voice" in the composition (melody, bass, accompaniment). Learn how to sing each part separately while "hearing" the other parts. Use the metronome. This ability will help you to maintain consistency, adding contrast, and accuracy in both composition and performance. Songs are comprised of overarching melodic themes, supported in the arrangement of bass and accompaniment. Learn how to *identify the structure* these themes take on in compositions. Identifying the structure can help you get "unstuck" when developing a piece: if you can see what you've done, that can help you see options for what to do next. Likewise, identifying structure can help you perfect a piece. It will help you check for balance and eliminate redundancy in sections.

Variation and repetition are the primary drivers of the thematic development of compositions. There are many processes for the development of these drivers—melodic iteration, sequential structuring, harmonic progression. Composers are always looking for a *balance between variation and repetition*. In guitar, this balance often involves exploring one's virtuosic potential in tandem with a well-supported and memorable melody.

When used as a means of *emphasizing* virtuosity, *motifs can be effective in augmenting themes*. But motifs, like "flashy technique," are no substitute for a great, well-arranged melody.

To *integrate extended techniques*, view them as supporting elements for your solo arrangements, and add them to the list of possibilities for portraying melody, bass, and rhythm.

COMPOSITION: INTERVIEWS WITH PIERRE BENSUSAN, LAURENCE JUBER, AND PETER FINGER

PIERRE BENSUSAN

Describe the considerations leading you to specialize in the DADGAD *tuning.*

Being self-taught on the guitar, I went away from the academic approach and have played several alternative tunings, which you can hear on my first two albums, *Près de Paris* and *2*. However, in 1978 I decided to stick with only one tuning in order to learn the fundamentals on the guitar, and chose *DADGAD*. The album *Musiques*, recorded in 1979, is my first recording using *DADGAD* throughout the album.

What are the advantages of the tuning?

I view *DADGAD* in the way most guitar players view standard tuning. I take as much advantage of its natural-sounding qualities, and yet can go away from it and play in any key, with no open string. The tuning is not the most crucial element; the inspiration, the ideas, and their translation into a guitaristic musical form, the organization and architecture of the music, the feel, the groove, the music itself… these are the keys. This tuning has certainly helped me to sound differently from any other guitarist and articulate and phrase differently, and have maybe more fun and understand what I had inside that wanted to come out. But sincerely, as much as *DADGAD* is now a natural extension of myself, I could have very well achieved the same or different results in standard tuning and have as much pleasure in the process. At the end of the day, the music is the guide, not the tuning. If you let the tuning control you, you will end up sounding like nothing.

How have you addressed limitations in your tuning, if they exist at all?

By deepening my approach to it—going away from the obvious fingerings and reflexes, following the music and not systematically what my fingers like to play. I have also worked on the agility of my left hand so that I could gradually address the stretching issues, which are more pronounced here because of these three strings tuned down one step and [therefore] a bit more sensitive to deal with here than in the standard-tuning context. All the chords, scales, modes, and all the rest of it, are there in an agreeable and playable form, which makes good ergonomic and sonic sense.

What strategies would you recommend to someone to acquire your level of fretboard knowledge in an open tuning they adopt?

I don't believe fretboard knowledge has anything to do with the tuning. Whatever the tuning you choose to play, ideally, you should know your way around as much as possible. It all has to do with the time you spend, the fun you have studying the fretboard, and the level of musicality that is inherent in each of us. As much as I rely on the fretboard and coincidences encountered when playing randomly my guitar, I rely even more strongly on my imagination and inner music to tell me what are the next notes I should play.

What fingering techniques do you use for solo lines? When generally do you use each combination of fingerings—such as p–i versus i–m or combinations of i–m–a—to execute your solo passages? And when do you use a thumb pick?

I started by always using a thumb pick and played the solo lines using the "lute technique," which is *p,i–p,m, p,i–p,m,* etc. Several years ago, I gradually changed my right-hand technique, and hardly use a thumb pick today. I play solo lines with picking or rest stroke techniques using *i-m-a* with my thumb often resting on one bass, as in flamenco. At times I would go back to lute technique as well, and use a combination of everything. I also use my little finger for chords which contain more than four voices, or roll my thumb on several bass strings.

Describe the importance of singing in developing and performing your music.

The voice is our first instrument. We always have it handy, and it could naturally be used to give a sound to any melodic, harmony, or bass line idea. Any voicing can be met and identified with the voice. It helps to bring the music inside.

What essential characteristics must a song have, in your opinion, for it to be great?

I am not sure I can describe in words what a song or music should have to be great. We see that, thank God, there is no recipe. But space, chant, movement, grace, dynamics, tempo, contrasts, unpredictability—and yet comfort—are essential qualities for the music to exist and find its bed.

It should be done in a sincere way, and one should not be preoccupied by any issue, result, or projection in the future other than the artistry and the music itself, whatever time it takes to produce it. As much as I have a hard time describing what the elements which put together a success are, I, like a lot of people who are not necessarily adept at an instrument, know right away when it's not working.

What creative techniques do you use to identify and develop your ideas?

I stay with my ideas a long time, in an inner circle, and feed them constantly. I also sing and accompany myself on the guitar; then I start to bring the elements on the guitar and decide then if the voice is still necessary or if the guitar can stand by itself.

How do you become unstuck?

By not thinking that I am stuck.

LAURENCE JUBER

What factors in your professional background and musical pursuits have influenced your approach to songwriting for guitar?

Being well grounded in music theory, 30 years of work as a studio musician, and having an obsessive quest for new sonority. I tend to think of myself as a composer with lousy keyboard skills who plays guitar both for a living and for recreation.

What essential characteristics must a song have, in your opinion, for it to be great?

A memorable tune.

Do the characteristics of a great tune differ at all if they are played as a fingerstyle guitar piece or arranged for some other context? If so, how?

The dynamics of an arrangement will change, but ultimately you still need a melodic hook that provides some emotional resonance for the listener.

What factors would lead you to choose developing or performing a piece in an open tuning versus standard tuning?

Register, texture, voicings, and such are all part of the guitaristic mystique. Sometimes I'll approach it as technical challenge, other times I'll just fall under the fingers. The ultimate criterion is whether it feels right.

What creative techniques do you use to identify and develop your ideas?

It's tough to capture that "first take" vibe with a fingerstyle piece that requires months of repetition to develop. Sometimes I'll record and transcribe my improvisations, but usually I'll seize on a musical motif and develop it harmonically and contrapuntally. Other times I'll be inspired by an event or an image and simply try to tell a story.

How do you become unstuck?

By doing things that are quite different from fingerstyle guitar. Musically, an orchestral session will give me a fresh perspective; some intense work composing a score, an electric blues jam. Getting away from the guitar helps, too. I'll do some "mental practice" and perhaps hear something that my fingers might not lead me to.

PETER FINGER

[Interview translated from German by the author.]
Describe the considerations leading you to specialize in the EBEGAD tuning.

It was a happenstance. At the time, around 1980, I was using around 15 different tunings.

One of them was *EBEGAD*. Because I wanted to begin improvising, 15 tunings were too many, so I started concentrating on this one. Since then, it's become my "standard tuning."

What are the advantages of your tuning?

There are neither advantages nor disadvantages. The tuning is simply different. The 4ths in the bass make chromatic runs difficult. The close intervals in the midrange [*E–G–A*] make large intervals difficult. The tonal characteristic of the tuning is, however, special and interesting—which can be said for all the other alternate tunings.

Are there any limitations to your tuning, and, if so, how have you addressed them?

No, there are not limitations, outside of the one higher note available in standard tuning.

How, specifically, did you build the knowledge of the fretboard that you have in your tuning?

I began as a beginner—note by note. Then, I wrote out the scales, then the chords.

What strategies would you recommend to someone to acquire your level of fretboard knowledge in an open tuning they adopt?

It's more about musical knowledge than the fretboard. That's what theory is for, and there are enough books available on the subject. After that, you can apply anything, regardless of the tuning you use. The more time you invest, the more you'll have it at your disposal. There are no secrets.

Your work involves the extensive use of blazing lead lines. When, generally, do you use each combination of fingers—such as p–i *versus* i–m *or combinations of* i–m–a—*to execute your solo passages?*

Because I use finger picks, I use *pi* [thumb/finger alteration] for all my passages. *ima* doesn't work so well with finger picks. I view *pi* technique as plectrum technique.

You listen to a lot of guitar music in your role as producer for Acoustic Music Records. What minimum requirements, compositionally, are you listening for when you are listening to something for consideration on your label? What essential characteristics must a song have, in your opinion, for it to be great?

There are so many differences. Someone with a blues background will compose differently from someone with a classical background. Both could be either very well or poorly conceived. Generally, it's good when there's something original to the material, or something packed with feeling. There are no recipes. One may be good rhythmically, the other harmonically, and the third one may have original melodies. All this can be good. And when it all comes together, then it's sensational.

CHAPTER 11

PRACTICE AND STAGE FRIGHT

PRACTICE

Making music involves the three major zones of human consciousness: the mind, the body, and the emotions. Effective practice involves techniques that reinforce key aspects in each zone with the help of focused repetition. The crucial elements of effective practice are clear goals; benchmarks for achieving those goals; a clear head; an uncluttered space in which to practice without disturbance; and . . .

. . . a *metronome*! Practice works because it helps the musician bring into play problem solving, visual memory, kinetic memory, and associations. Your metronome is an invaluable tool for rehearsing trouble spots, analyzing passages, and even mapping thoughts and feelings in relation to particular phrases.

Your confidence can also greatly improve by repetitively practicing sections that "scare you." One lesser-known trick is to practice the piece at a tempo slightly faster than you plan to perform it. The reason? When we're nervous in performance settings, adrenaline flows and our heart rate increases. Since we subconsciously associate the tempo of a piece with our heart rate, it's best to be able to cover the calibrated margin should the need arise when sitting in front of an audience.

Cognitive Reinforcement Through Practice	
Mind	Analyzing, problem solving, memorizing
Body	Visually memorizing, kinetically memorizing
Emotions	Actively associating music with images and feelings

Structural analysis and harmonic analysis, described in this book as the separation of voices (see Chapter 10, Composition and Creativity), are key elements in effective practice. The simple act of recognizing the voices, sections, and phrases in a composition is a form of practice, as it reinforces an intellectual "snapshot" for the performance.

Learning to sing, play, and hear each voice helps tremendously with troubleshooting. Isolating problematic spots requires the ability to work with voices in isolation. We need to be able to hear whether the part is in the melody, the accompaniment, or the bass so that we can work on it and get it right through practice. Training our "mind's ear" to hear each voice separately helps us identify trouble spots effectively.

Memorization

There is also another aspect of cognition reinforced through practice: memorization. Memorization in music is predominantly aural, but also visual; that is, we remember not only what we hear but what we see. Visual memorization is often neglected in practice. This form of practice involves using your mind to "see" yourself play. Think about it: In your memory of a piece, can you go to a particular measure and know *exactly* which fingering you are using on *exactly* which fret? Can you envision the entire piece linearly, such that you can see what is going to be played 16 or 32 measures later? This kind of memory implies intimate knowledge of a piece of music, and goes way beyond simply "knowing how the song goes."

The "muscle memory" aspect of practice is familiar to most of us. When we practice, we in essence automate the physical behavior—the sequence of finger, hand, and arm motions—involved in a piece. When learning a piece, you play it slowly until it's "under the fingers." (This is done in tandem with a metronome. If there's a trouble spot, isolate it, using analysis, and practice it slowly with a metronome until you can play it.)

Emotions and Associations

Do not neglect the emotional dimension. Try to stay clear-headed and avoid distractions when you practice. The mind makes its own associations; if you're watching TV while you practice, it might conjure up a rerun of *NYPD Blue* when you're performing. A player is far better off creating their own mental and aural images while practicing. What is the story you associate with the piece? What feelings and emotions come up for you when playing it?

Performance is an act of *transference*. It's good to know what you associate and feel in the piece, and practice it with that in mind. That way, when you perform, the odds are that it will be easier for you to transmit those thoughts and associations to your audience. Moreover, if you get nervous, reflecting on those thoughts may help remind you why you decided to put all that effort into learning the piece in the first place!

STAGE FRIGHT

"It doesn't matter what the audience thinks. What matters is what you *think."*
—Ralph Towner

As David Byrne once said, "Sometimes it all works out. Sometimes I'm a little freaked out." We have all experienced stage fright at some point. But if we have stage fright regularly, how do we mitigate against its effects?

Stage fright affects the brain, the emotions, and the body. Your mind becomes preoccupied with irrational thoughts regarding audience reception and your ability (or perceived inability) to play key sections that have troubled you in practice. You react emotionally to these thoughts by becoming afraid. Your body reacts to the emotional response with increased heart rate and clammy, sometimes shaky hands. If things get really bad, this circle of reaction feeds back upon itself. Your physical reaction magnifies the mental source of concern, making for an even stronger emotional reaction, which makes your heart beat even faster. It's a vicious, panicky cycle. What are you going to do about this?

There are three ways to deal with stage fright: knowing the true nature of the performance setting, relying on memory, and trusting in the efficacy of practice. Let's look closely at all three.

The True Nature of the Performance Setting

The likelihood is high that when performing, especially early in your career, you will be nervous at some point. It's also common to be more nervous at the *beginning* of a performance. This is a completely natural response to the performance setting, which is mitigated with experience and diminishes naturally over the course of the performance. The simple acknowledgment of these facts goes a long way in addressing stage fright. You can expect it—but also expect it not to last the whole performance.

One way to diminish the effects of stage fright is to be aware of common cognitive distortions that come with the territory.

Confusing Fear with Nervousness. When you're on stage, it's easy to believe that because you *feel* nervous you *are* nervous. It's an emotional fallacy, a trick of the mind. Just because you are nervous does not mean you are *afraid*. It actually may mean you're *excited*. Excitement is related physiologically to fear, but it's not the same thing. If you're excited about performing, enjoy it!

Magnification/Minimization. When onstage, thoughts and perceptions can become magnified, resulting in the potential for distortion. For example, a small microphone suddenly seems *really* big. Likewise, those small problems you had with the piece can suddenly seem really big as well. You can find yourself thinking, *Here comes the section where I always miss that note. I can't miss it this time! Everyone will think I'm no good and….*

Many of our performance fears relate to magnifying trivial problems or not trusting our own practice routines. But, this thinking doesn't reflect the reality of the performance setting. The odds are, if you miss a note, or do something wrong, probably no one will notice. It seems like a big deal to you, because you worked 40 hours to get that piece just right, and focused on every minuscule detail. However, if you practice effectively, you probably won't make many mistakes. And, the errors you do make just might highlight for the audience what you are doing *right*. As one fan once put it to me, "You are so damned on-the-mark that I don't notice it sometimes *unless* you make a mistake!" When you see yourself heading in this direction mentally, recognize it but don't become entangled in it.

Reading the Audience's Mind. One very common irrational fear performers have is that an audience won't like them. There is, in fact, no way to know how an audience is going to receive your show. However, it's most likely that they will like it. Why?

Here is the biggest secret about performance: the audience has a strong, vested interest in liking you because it's a form of self-validation for them to do so. The truth is, you'd practically have to insult your audience to get them *not* to like you. Attending a live performance is not like being a prisoner to an in-flight movie or being victimized by elevator music. The people in the audience have *chosen to see you* and sometimes even pay money to do so! There is no real way to predict what people will think of your performance. However, in all likelihood, they will probably think it's pretty good. The bottom line is, you shouldn't worry about it. If someone doesn't like your song, maybe they'll like your performance. If they don't care for your performance, they still may like your song. Remember that there is a big gap between what you think and what they think. In the end, it's up to you to do your personal best—and only you are the judge of that. Hey, isn't being onstage something you thought was the greatest thing in the world, and that's why you wanted to do it? If so, you might as well treat yourself right and bask in the experience.

Relying on Memory

Relying on memory is one of the best things you can do to deal with stage fright. By the time you make it to the stage, you will have practiced the pieces over and over again. They are in your muscle memory. If you're nervous, think back on the feelings and images you associate with the piece. The more you do this in practice, the easier it will be to do onstage. Revisiting your associations has a twofold effect. First, it takes your mind *off* the thoughts causing you anxiety. Second, it refocuses your attention on what you want to communicate to the audience. So, this approach represents a win-win!

But, let's say you encounter a situation where your muscle memory doesn't serve you. In that case, fall back on your *visual memory*. If you get "lost," there's no need for a train wreck. Keep playing. The worst that can happen is you forget a few bars. Call up your visual memory and use it to jump to the next note, phrase, or section.

Trusting in the Efficacy of Practice

As my friends will tell you, I'm a nervous, high-strung guy. In fact, I'm a "paranoid perfectionist." No matter how much I practice, I'm still scared when I go onstage.

So I've developed a motto: *It doesn't matter if I'm scared, as long as I'm prepared.* Part of what performance is all about is the joy that comes with the unexpected. Regard the unknown as an eventuality and learn to love it—because the outcome is never what you expect. As long as you're prepared, and can fall back on these recovery methods, the odds are you'll do just fine. In fact, it's hard to lose.

APPENDIX

BUILDING FRETBOARD KNOWLEDGE IN ALTERED TUNINGS

Players like Pierre Bensusan, Michael Hedges, Peter Finger, Peppino D'Agostino, and Don Ross have shown that altered tunings can be just as versatile as standard tuning. Since the familiar voicings and fingerings of standard are not easily accessed in open tunings, a new tuning can awaken the intuition and lead to unexpected new ideas. However, effectively completing musical ideas in altered tunings requires the building of fretboard knowledge. With enough practice and experimentation, a player can explore the full potential of a tuning and the mix of fretted and open strings it offers.

SCALING DOWN

While developing melodic and harmonic ideas in an altered tuning, find the scales that are in the melody's key and learn how to play them fluently in the altered tuning. Then, find the harmonic cadences that underlie them. You'll want to explore the scales and harmonies not just in one position, but all over the neck. Figuring out how to extend the scales and cadences across the fretboard will help guide you to broaden your melodic ideas beyond the confines of a few frets.

The exercises in this section are provided to help you "pull back the curtain" on altered tunings so that you can play and compose as knowledgeably as you might in standard.

Ex. A-1   *D Major in DADGAD*

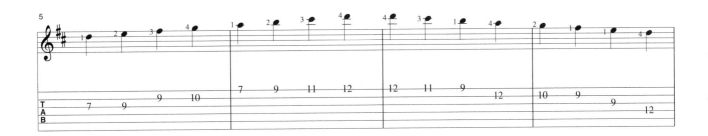

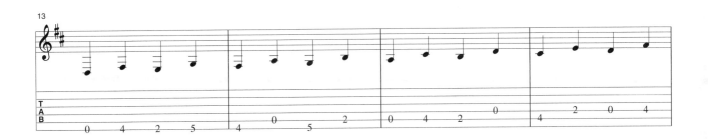

example continues...

Ex. A-1 continued

Ex. A-2   *D Minor in DADGAD*

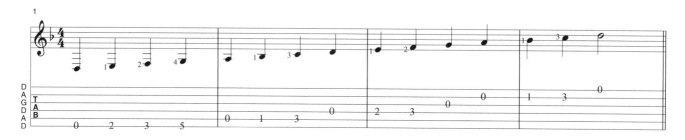

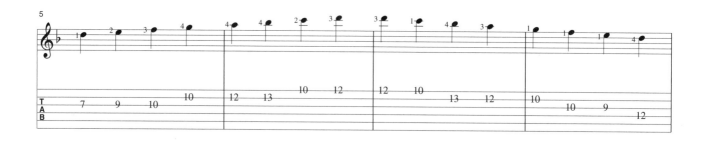

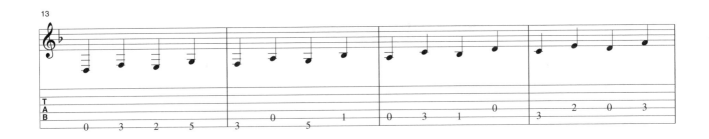

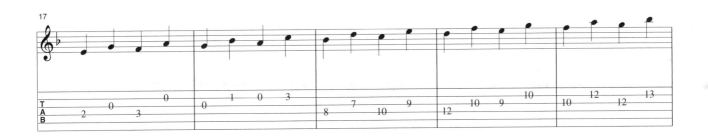

example continues...

Ex. A-2 continued

Ex. A-3   Second-Position *G* Major in *DADGAD*

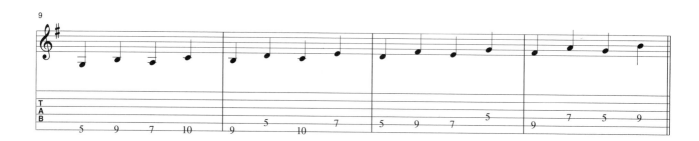

For this example use *p-i* finger alternation and maintain the fret-hand finger pattern given for each string unless indicated otherwise.

Ex. A-4   Second-Position *G* Minor in *DADGAD*

example continues...

Ex. A-4 continued

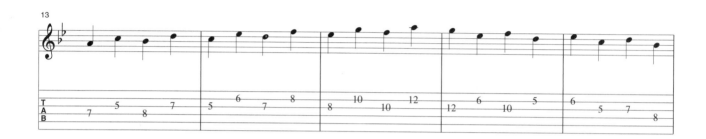

When you play this example use the fingerings from previous exercises as a guide to devising your own fingerings and alternating patterns.

Ex. A-5   *C Pentatonic Scale and Arpeggios in CGCGCD*

Ex. A-6 Whole-Step Scale and Arpeggios in *EBEGAD*

Ex. A-7   Minor Cadences in _DADGAD_

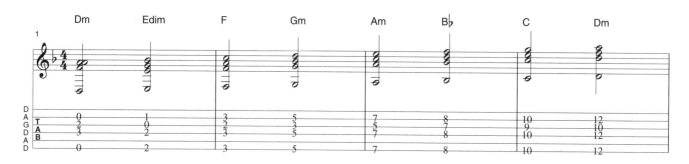

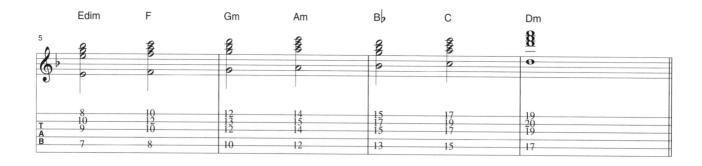

Ex. A-8   5th, 7th, 9th, and 11th Cadences in _DADGAD_

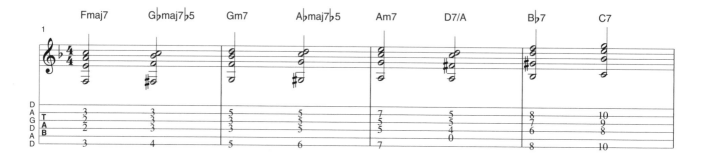

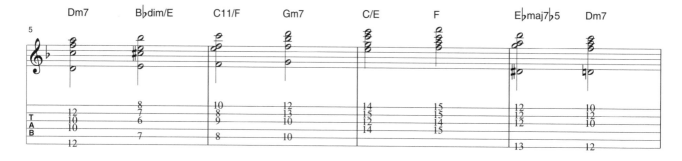

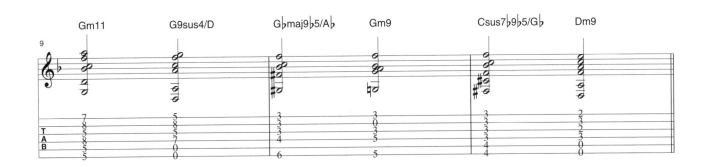

Ex. A-9   Major Cadences in *CGCGCD*

Ex. A-10 Minor Cadences in *CGCGCD*

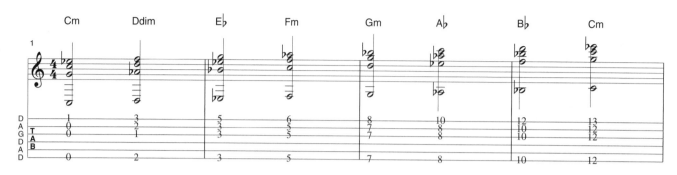

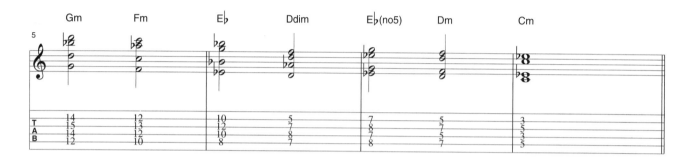

Consider, as you tackle the first examples, how you might further explore scales, arpeggios, and harmonies on your own. Now that you have the major and minor scales and arpeggios in *DADGAD*, can you form them for *CGCGCD* and *EBEGAD*? Can you form the whole-step and pentatonic scale in *DADGAD* and *EBEGAD*?

Chord formation and voicing possibilities are also unique to each tuning. The chordal examples here provide the *DADGAD* and *CGCGCD* cadences used in the pieces featured in this book, such as "These Days" and "Dee Dum" in Chapter 9. For extra credit, try to find major and minor cadences in *EBEGAD*. As you can see, anything is possible.

ABOUT THE AUTHOR

Brian Gore performs as the founder of International Guitar Night (IGN/USA), and is an endorser of LR Baggs amplification and Ryan Guitars. He can also be found touring solo as well as on double bills in concert halls and festivals around the world. He's been featured on NPR's nationally syndicated *Echoes Radio* and has performed live on many NPR affiliate stations.

His recording *Legacy* (Acoustic Music Records) features solo works and duets with Grammy-winner Andrew York, Peppino D'Agostino, and others. He also appears solo and in musical collaboration in the Steve Vai's Favored Nations release, *An Evening with International Guitar Night Live: Featuring Pierre Bensusan, Andrew York, Guinga, and Brian Gore.*

Brian's website is www.guitarpoet.com.

PHOTO CREDITS

Page 7 (Pierre Bensusan): Txema Rojo.
Page 7 (Laurence Juber): Kenna Love.
Page 7 (Martin Taylor): Norman McMillan.
Page 8 (Laurence Juber): courtesy Laurence Juber.
Page 8 (Don Ross): Christine Smyth.
Page 8 (Peppino D'Agostino): Giorgio Uccellini.

ON THE CD

WHEN IT COMES TO MUSIC, WE WROTE THE BOOK.

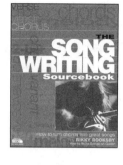
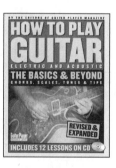
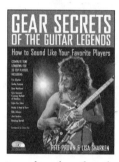
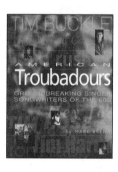
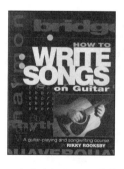